# EMBODIED HEALING

*for Silke*

## USING YOGA TO RECOVER FROM TRAUMA AND EXTREME STRESS

LISA DANYLCHUK, LMFT

## Copyright

Cover Design: John Matthews

Interior & Back Cover Design: Jennifer Stimson

Editing: Grace Kerina

WOT Diagram: Lisa Danylchuk

Author's photo courtesy of Coriander Stasi

# ADVANCE PRAISE

"I've been in the helping profession for 20 years, and when I attend lectures on counseling-related issues, I generally don't expect to learn new information that challenges my own theory of change so much so that it makes me reassess my own practice. Lisa came to speak on trauma-informed counseling to my class of graduate students a few weeks ago, and I'm still reeling from her innovative approach to trauma, wondering how much disservice I've done to my former clients by not approaching their treatment with a trauma-informed lens. Lisa's book is sure to leave you in similar introspection. This is a must-read for any clinician who provides services to populations impacted by trauma."

– JOSEPHINE M. KIM, PHD, LMHC, NCC, FACULTY, HARVARD GRADUATE SCHOOL OF EDUCATION, AUTHOR OF *THE SECRET TO CHILDREN'S SELF-ESTEEM* **AND** *SELF-ESTEEM IN THE CLASSROOM*

"As our collective understanding of the mind-body connection deepens, it is essential that teachers and healers understand the bridges connecting yoga and trauma recovery. Yogis and mental health professionals alike have a wealth of information that, when pooled, can offer massive opportunities for the mind and body to find union and heal together. In this book, Lisa Danylchuk - who has studied and practiced with me for over 15 years - outlines foundations in yoga philosophy and trauma recovery that all therapists and yoga teachers should know. This book does a great service to healers holding space for others and to those looking to move through their own challenging life circumstances. I highly recommend it for anyone seeking to support a world that fosters peace, healing and empowerment through mindful movement."

– SEANE CORN, YOGA TEACHER AND CO-FOUNDER OF OFF THE MAT, INTO THE WORLD ®

"*Embodied Healing* seamlessly and accessibly integrates trauma theory and yoga philosophy. This book helps yoga teachers and healing professionals understand the layered complexity of trauma and its impact, and offers a solid foundation for how yoga can foster lasting change. These days, the need for trauma-informed practice is strong, and this book provides a conscious, clear road map for those in a position to help."

– ELENA BROWER, AUTHOR OF *ART OF ATTENTION*

"Lisa brings her wealth and depth of knowledge to the subject of how to use yoga as method and means for transformational healing. I have worked with her in a variety contexts and have seen firsthand her capacity to couple compassion with a clear, grounded, and practical approach to many of the challenges that arise in the classroom."

– CARRIE OWERKO, SENIOR CERTIFIED IYENGAR TEACHER AND LABAN MOVEMENT ANALYST

"In this book, Lisa brilliantly illustrates the power of yoga, both philosophy and asana, coupled with clear science for profound emotional healing. Her unique voice of deep experience of heartbreak and her years of study and practice in psychology and the art of yoga creates an accessible and amazingly detailed guide to healing. This book is essential for any seeker of healing as well as for teachers, guides, and facilitators in all fields."

– MELANIE SALVATORE-AUGUST, ERYT500/PRYT, AUTHOR OF
*KITCHEN YOGA: SIMPLE HOME PRACTICES TO TRANSFORM MIND,
BODY AND LIFE*

"Lisa Danylchuk is a brilliant yoga teacher and therapist bridging the worlds of yoga and psychology. Thanks to her pioneering interest in these two fields, she offers us a clear and understandable path using yoga as means of recovering from the pain of trauma. With sincerity, humor, and knowledge Lisa shares the tools to help us understand ourselves and others more fully and completely. Read this book!"

– NIKKI ESTRADA, YOGA TEACHER TRAINER, MOTHER,
SPIRITUAL ENTHUSIAST

"Lisa has taken the latest knowledge about trauma and integrated it with her training and experience with yoga. She's been taught by the best in both fields, and that is rare. She speaks honestly, with respect for the reader, giving support while sharing what she has learned about working through trauma, completely – body, mind, and spirit."

– LYNETTE S. DANYLCHUK, PHD, PRESIDENT OF THE INTERNATIONAL
SOCIETY FOR THE STUDY OF TRAUMA AND DISSOCIATION

# TABLE OF
# CONTENTS

# INTRODUCTION

If you've picked up this book, chances are you're a special kind of healer. You've seen some serious challenges, been obliterated by life, had your mind, heart, or even house explode and you have marched on, putting it all back together. Congratulations! You're a walking testament to human resilience and a shining light to those in the world who desperately want to follow in your footsteps as they journey through their own challenges.

Being a special kind of healer means you have been wounded or have struggled, as all of us have, in unique ways. Thanks to ongoing studies about trauma and healing, there are specific things we can do and attitudes we can cultivate to promote our own and others' healing. You may already have found some of these helpful as you've traveled your own path.

Those of us who have overcome trauma often initially find ways of coping that, while they may help momentarily, create other problems or don't create lasting positive change. This book shares methods of healing that can help foster long-term, integrated healing – the kind that builds momentum and the capacity not only for more healing, but for deep, soulful joy.

Look around. Can you identify a single human being in your environment who you're sure has never suffered?

Do you know anyone who doesn't have a deep desire for happiness? This is a central aspect of human experience: we suffer, and yet we strive. Trauma overwhelms us and brings uncomfortable internal experiences, which lead us to want to avoid our thoughts and feelings. Trauma changes our experience of thought, emotion, and sense of being in our bodies. Suffering is universal, and yet nobody teaches us how to cope with this truth of life. If we're lucky, we find a wise mentor, parent, or friend – someone who has waded through the muck of trauma and emerged enriched, whole, and inspired – and we are able to take their hand.

This book extends that hand to you to support you on your continued path of healing, and on your path as healer. If you work as a yoga teacher, mental health professional, or in related healing arts, this book will give you tools to understand and cultivate practices that support healing. If you want to infuse your current life and work with more meaning, depth, and purpose, this is the book for you. In it, I offer simple, practical, noninvasive principles that support trauma recovery. I give explanations about how we can use yoga, and why yogic practices are an ideal complement to trauma recovery work.

Trauma often involves loss – of life, of opportunity, of a sense of safety or protection – and yet, as a result of their traumatic experience, many people also experience a profound shift in the ways they look at life. I invite you to join me on this path, and offer all the healing you can, even if you are still in the process of healing.

I'm a yoga instructor and psychotherapist and the effects of trauma are often very visible to me, but many consider trauma to be an invisible disease. True, there are no purple bruises, no broken bones to measure psychological trauma (although, unfortunately, physical and psychological trauma can occur simultaneously). Often, however, we don't see the ways those around us suffer. Psychological trauma can be tucked away, hidden behind shame, secrecy, privacy, and – for some people – easily masked by a smiling face.

Adverse Childhood Experiences (ACEs) include physical, emotional, and sexual abuse and neglect, and are common initiators of post-traumatic stress. Every year, more than three million reports of child abuse are made in the United States, involving more than six million children. The US loses an average of between four and seven children every day who die from child abuse and neglect. (Felitti et al, 1998). We've learned that adverse childhood experiences are predictors not only of post-traumatic stress disorder (PTSD), but also of impacted physical health outcomes across a lifetime (Harris, 2014).

About five million Americans suffer from PTSD during their lifetime, and approximately 7.5 percent of Americans will experience PTSD in their lifetime. People with PTSD often experience depression and other mental health challenges. Women are twice as likely to experience PTSD as men. War veterans, law enforcement officers, firefighters, and EMT workers are particularly vulnerable to PTSD, and anyone with PTSD is at a high risk for suicide (Caruso, 2015).

Post-traumatic stress is commonly associated with military vets, and for good reason. According to the RAND Center for Military Health Policy Research, at least twenty percent of Iraq and Afghanistan veterans have PTSD and/or depression, 50 percent of those with PTSD do not seek treatment, and – out of the half who do seek treatment – only half of those people get "minimally adequate" treatment (Tanielian & Jaycox, 2008). In addition, the US Defense Department and the US Veterans Administration together spend $3.3 billion annually on medications and therapies meant to curb or cure PTSD, yet they have no evidence to support the effectiveness of these treatments on veterans (Briggs, 2014).

Perhaps you know someone who has lost, or is at risk of losing, their life to post-traumatic stress. Some trauma survivors choose to take life into their own hands and end it. Others stay physically alive but fail to reconnect with their emotional and spiritual selves, and some people with PTSD struggle for years to find a therapy that will work for them. While most trauma survivors go through dark days and nights, it is possible to make it through – to rehabilitate your body, mind, and emotions, and to nurse your spirit back to health.

## A New World of Healing

Ask any beauty pageant contestant – world peace would be really, really sweet. The vast majority of humanity would cheer to see a world without suffering, without the experience or effects of trauma on ourselves or others. While I cannot single-handedly eliminate child abuse, end war, or prevent trauma from occurring in the world, I do know how to help mitigate the effects of extreme stress and trauma, and that is what you will learn about in the pages to come. This book supports the vision that healing is possible, and aims to help you find ways to access your own healing potential and become a catalyst for others to join you on the ride.

Armed with tools founded in yoga philosophy and trauma theory, we can learn to cope with stress in order to mitigate the effects of trauma, improve health, reduce violence, and prevent the tragedies that occur in extreme cases of PTSD. Sadly, when we lose someone as a result of post-traumatic stress, their loved ones absorb the effects of trauma as they experience the loss, and they're faced with recovering from their own experience of unexpected, incomprehensible change. Without intervention, this cycle of trauma continues, widening its reach.

Many people, agencies, and governments justify not investing in PTSD prevention simply because we can't measure the effects of what doesn't occur. This logic has always failed me, because we *can* measure what does occur. Rather than focusing on what's being reduced, we can focus on – and measure – what we're cultivating: health, peace, healing, recovery, integration, and wellness. These are as measurable in people recovering with PTSD as they are in people facing any other mental disorder. Our perspective is slowly re-orienting to build the instruments necessary to assess health, not just disease.

My vision for the world is that we open our minds wide enough to fathom that happiness, joy, and health are, in fact, our birthright, and that we can work to cultivate environments, circumstances, and cultures that support our ability to cope with the inevitable cycles of stress and thriving. As an example, the nation of Bhutan measures its success in Gross National Happiness, rather than Gross National Product. For us as a society to move toward greater health, it takes a shift of values and perspective, a re-ordering of what we measure, what we chose to invest in and the goals we choose to work toward.

I also envision a world in which we open our hearts so wide we recognize our intimate connections to each other and to our shared humanity. We can stand in others' shoes and have compassion for journeys and struggles of those whose lives are different than ours. We can support each other in thriving, rather than competing, acquiring, seeking to dominate, or hoarding due to our fears. We can come to a place where we share what helps us heal, and we encourage others to do the same.

## My Vision for You

My vision for you, dear reader, is that you cultivate a deeper understanding of trauma, resilience, and how to cultivate yourself as a leader in the healing movement. By the end of this book, I hope you feel joyful, inspired, and armed with all the information you need to support yourself in bringing more life into your own experience and into the world at large. In this way, you can help to create a ripple effect of health and wholeness in the world.

Perhaps this sounds lofty to you. Perhaps you have, at times, like many of us, felt unready or unable to make such an impact. Maybe you feel a sense of lack and think you need more education, power, money, or energy to lead others in healing. You may feel that you have so much on your own plate that you can't also bear the weight of helping others. Or you may have thought, "Who am I to tell someone else what to do?" You may have those doubts, but, even so, please don't underestimate the power of your presence in this world, in your life, and in others' lives.

In this book, I'll cover the basics of modern trauma recovery theory, yoga philosophy, and how to apply the two in practice. I'll discuss trauma and the body, yoga's solutions to trauma, resilience, relationships, as well as systemic challenges and solutions to teaching yoga to traumatized populations. I'll wrap up by addressing issues of sustainability and self-care for healers, and explore how to deal with obstacles that come up along the way in this work.

This book will show you the *how* and *why* of trauma recovery. It outlines the tools, concepts, and issues you need to be aware of when teaching those with PTSD – tools that will help you grow and will help your students find healing. My hope is that this book will give you the confidence to step forward and claim your healing power.

# CHAPTER 1

## My Story

You may be asking yourself why you're so interested in trauma and healing. I've asked myself this many times. Although I was born to two therapists (one specializing in trauma and dissociation, the other a marriage family therapist and Vietnam veteran) and have had Vedic astrologers tell me there are "yogas for yoga" in my chart (patterns indicating I would be interested in yoga), I have also been thrown into the fire myself. I, too, have experienced trauma.

Like you, I have seen dark days, reconciled losses, dealt with violence, and made my way through things I wish had never happened. Without belaboring my own story, I want you to understand that I've experienced unexpected and deep heartbreak, and – in many ways – have been blessed by it. You can easily find more about my personal stories online and through my website **http://www.howwecanheal.com**, where I've shared them openly. Rather than focus right now on the stories of my own struggle and what brought me pain, I want you to understand my internal experiences following my personal experience of trauma.

In the wake of traumatic loss, after my older brother died suddenly and unexpectedly, my heart was cracked open. At that point in my life, I was a busy bee of a college student and my plate was full. My natural reaction in response to losing one of the dearest and deepest connections I had known, was to stop, grieve, and pare down. I chose to release all that was unnecessary so that what was most necessary could speak, and what wanted to speak was love.

What had been an hour-long weekly commitment to tutoring youth in a Los Angeles housing development became a focal point for me. Rather than over-filling my schedule by teaching an extra kickboxing or dance class, or double majoring ("doin' too much," as the kids used to call it), I dedicated my time to cultivating relationships and programs that would support the youth I'd been serving through the UCLA Watts Tutorial Program. Before my own experience of loss, I knew I really liked those kids; afterwards, I discovered I had loved them all along.

I don't say this to try to paint myself as a Mother Theresa. I say it to share the deep experience of love that came with my loss. Grief, yes. Overwhelm, yes. Confusion, all the time. But also love, love, love. I loved those kids, and they knew it. They felt it. I loved them because I knew that they had seen all the pain I had, and more, and they were still there. The spark of resilience in them was so strong it encouraged my own flame of healing to grow.

It's common to hear people in the helping professions saying they get more than they give, and my early experiences of working with youth dealing with the effects of complex trauma were no exception. Even remembering it now opens and warms my heart. I kept in touch with some of those students for a decade, and have since lost touch with them. I can guarantee that, at some level, they knew and felt the love I had for them, and it fueled our healing relationship.

My point is that in the wake of my own devastation, there was love. Immense oceans of it. There was so much love it filled my shocked body and initiated a process of healing.

Yoga was central to my recovery from trauma. I went to yoga classes and worked through anger, sadness, tension, and collapse. I worked through nostalgia, memory, and spiritual questions. I offered my practice to my late brother, and I felt him with me. I found a deep, lasting sense that all was, indeed, well, and that, at my core, I was love, he was love, and we could never be without each other, even in death.

That may sound dramatic to you – unless you have felt it. Whether or not you've lost someone close to you, I suspect that, since you're reading this book, you've endured and you've felt this energy of love within yourself, in your relationships, or in your experience of life.

Throughout this book, do not let this feeling go. This feeling is your ticket to healing. This energy of love is what we need to cultivate in order to heal. This is what fills us with life and purpose, and what motivates us to go on. I firmly believe that healing is a function and a manifestation of love.

I figured out how to recover from trauma by letting all but the most essential pieces of my life fall away. Yoga was one of those essential pieces. Doing yoga was not always a pleasant process, but it gave me a container for my grief, my injury, my deep and sometimes conflicting emotions. It gave me moments of faith and trust that, despite evidence to the contrary, all was well and I was okay. Through yoga, I found moments of peace, and the more I practiced, the more those feelings became my foundation for life.

I know what it's like to feel deep pain and soul-crushing loss, and to navigate through to a cultivation of peace and joy. In my work as psychotherapist and yoga instructor, I help people who fear becoming stuck in their pain see that those emotions can be two sides to the same coin, that opening to the grief, overwhelm, anger, confusion, and muck can also open us to love and the truth of who we are.

I used to say that before my brother passed my life was a puzzle, with me slowly putting the pieces into place where they fit, and then losing him was like water pouring water over the whole puzzle, throwing it all in a blender, and tossing the contents around the room. My task seemed impossible. How could I ever put the puzzle of my life back together? I resolved to take the new substance, the soggy material I now had, with its mishmash of colors and textures, and create something completely new with it.

I've always loved impressionist paintings. What I'd like to think I've created with my puzzle-sludge is an impressionistic piece that's more art than science, that conveys to those observing how light looks and feels, that gives a sense of texture and dimension. I'd like to think that because of my own experience with loss, my heart and soul shine through my skin even more now. This shift has changed who I am as a person, but it has enhanced me, not depleted me. Before my brother died, I was already studying integrative health. The experiences I went through when he died fueled a depth of understanding no degree could have offered or delivered.

Having been a counselor, yoga teacher, and psychotherapist over the course of the last fifteen years, I've had the privilege of being with people who've shared the truth of their human experience with me. I've seen people move, breathe, grieve, express, and lighten their loads. I'm convinced that yoga, in it's broadest sense, and as you will come to understand it through this book, has something for everyone. Opportunities for healing are everywhere, and the practice of yoga is rich with them. For anyone who seeks it, there is to be found in yoga a practice, a principle, an insight, a discovery that facilitates resilience.

Connect, move, breathe. You are not alone. The pain does pass, and there are ways to process and cope with overwhelming memories, thoughts, sensations, and emotions. There is someone out there who wants to hold your hand, whose soul will be satisfied by doing so. Find them. Reach out to them. Ask to be held in your time of need and, when you're ready to do so, reach out your own arms to those who need you. This is how we evolve as a species, through love. This is how we put an end to trauma, violence, and suffering. We connect in love, steeping ourselves into it and putting it out into the world with our very presence.

This is who you are and what you will do, should you choose a path of healing. Everything in this book is here to guide you and support you in connecting with love, in love, to heal and help others heal from trauma. This book is a guide for your healing journey.

# CHAPTER 2

## Understanding Trauma

### What is trauma?

Before we go any further, we need to define our terms. While the word trauma often summons a mental picture of war, natural disaster, and other such crises, it has also become a common word to toss into casual conversation. That haircut? So traumatizing. Did you see the way that clerk treated me? I'm traumatized! Blind date? Recipe for post-traumatic stress. Given the way the word trauma is thrown around in conversation these days, it can become a nebulous task to draw the line and define what is and what is not, in fact, traumatic.

Before we move forward, I want you to be prepared; the information I present in this chapter is the densest material in the book. In essence, you're starting off your run uphill. I'm a runner a well as a yogini, but you don't need to run an ultra marathon to know that it's challenging to start a run uphill. The good news is that it's downhill after this, so the material will get easier to digest as we go. In this chapter, we build a foundation for all that is to come. Invest time and attention here and you'll coast through the rest.

I also want you to be prepared that studying trauma can bring up your own defenses, your own ways of coping with intense emotions. Notice yourself and your reactions throughout this book – and also as you do your work with people who are in the process of healing. Do you get sleepy? Do you become agitated, or fast-forward to the future? Notice the habits of your mind and the experiences in your body. They can help inform your own healing.

In this chapter, we talk a lot about trauma. Just the word can bring up associations in your mind and trigger reactions. So notice, do you get fidgety or distracted? Do you get self-deprecating or critical? Do you get super happy and giggly? Reactions to trauma need not be challenging or negative. Just notice your state as we go through this material, and particularly if you feel like that you're zoning out or disconnecting from it take a pause, reconnect and come back. This is an ongoing practice.

Building your awareness of your reactions doesn't mean you have to force yourself to connect with and process all the emotions present at once. Simply notice what arises within you. It will help to acknowledge, "Something's happening here." From there, you can choose what bites to chew now and how you can best self-regulate. Get comfortable and challenge yourself to stay present, alert, and connected. Ask yourself, "How is this information helping me?" Remember that this is about you working with your clients, about your students growing. This is about helping them become lighter or happier. It's about healing. Keep that in mind as we wade through these definitions.

## Textbook PTSD

Given the potential for confusion, let's define our terms. Post-traumatic stress disorder (PTSD), in its textbook form, involves a brush with death or violence and includes the following experiences, drawn from the Diagnostic and Statistical Manual of Mental Disorders, or DSM-5 (APA, 2013):

- Intrusions
- Avoidance
- Negative changes in thought and mood
- Changes in physiological arousal and reactivity

PTSD can occur because of something that happens directly to us, by witnessing something traumatic, or even by hearing a traumatic story about something that happened to a loved one or a stranger. PTSD can occur if we're exposed to trauma in the course of our jobs (for example, if an ER nurse loses a patient while trying to resuscitate them, or a social worker hears about children's struggles all day).

Before we go further, let's break down the four categories of experiences listed above, to clarify and understand these classic symptoms of post-traumatic stress.

## Intrusions

Intrusions are, most simply put, reactions coming to you that you're not consciously choosing. Intrusions can be thoughts, feelings, or physiological reactions that are reminiscent of or relevant to the original trauma. They occur when anything – an image, smell, memory, emotion, or body sensation – comes into your awareness uninvited.

Have you ever had a memory of an embarrassing moment and shuddered or squirmed at the thought? Like that time I was seven and dropped a pair of my underwear on the floor in front of my brothers and their friends while they were playing ping pong. We often shudder at the thought of how embarrassed we were in the past. When you can't get that thought out of your head or have nightmares about it, we can this an intrusion. If you feel a shudder when you call up the memory, or if you have a physical response even when you're not thinking about it, you could be experiencing a somatic, or physical, intrusion.

As you can see, intrusions come in many forms. Nightmares, endless thoughts about a memory or experience, unwanted negative feelings, and even physical sensations. When – no matter how hard you try – you can't prevent a thought from reoccurring, you're likely experiencing an intrusion.

# Avoidance

On to the next criteria, stay with me! Avoidance is our tendency to look away from the uncomfortable. We often avoid thoughts or feelings if they feel too big to address in the moment. Sometimes the desire to avoid comes from a place of wisdom because the feeling or experience is too much for the whole of the body's system to feel all at once. Other times, we could look at the issue, but simply don't want to, or don't believe we're able to, face our uncomfortable feelings.

Even if a thought about something small upsets you, you may have a mental habit of pushing it aside or, as a dear friend of mine conceptualizes it, putting it in the filing cabinet. Organizing your thoughts is great, but if you never open the filing cabinet or it's leaking its emotional contents out subconsciously, that will become a problem.

One thing I've learned from being a psychotherapist is that we can sweep our feelings around, re-arrange, reorganize, and play tricks on them, but we can't deny them. Typically, the more we run or fight with our emotions, the louder they'll speak. Avoidance can also be an amazing gift. It shows us that there's something big happening. Once we recognize our avoidance, we know there's a strong emotion or reaction present. We can then choose to listen. Attention has amazing healing power. When we bring our full attention to our experience, we can watch our experience transform.

Changes in mood and thoughts are also very common in the wake of trauma. You may find your mind hijacked with potential solutions related to the traumatic experience – things you could have, would have, or should have done. (Even if you've learned from your experience and now know that you would do it differently the next time around, please stop *should*ing on yourself!). Thoughts may seem to go faster, slower, or be pulled in specific directions. You also may find your mood changing frequently or getting stuck in a funky state. These are common aspects of life after trauma and can be a challenge to deal with, not only for the person experiencing them but also for those looking to give support. Changes in mood can impact our availability and our felt sense of connection in relationships.

## Arousal and Reactivity

What happens when you're driving and someone slams on the brakes in front of you? Our bodies respond to life-threatening situations with a surge of energy, sometimes with collapse or shut down or by developing a vigilant protective mechanism to try to prevent such a trauma from ever happening again. When a difficult situation arises, our bodies mobilize to respond; sometimes we use that energy to do something physical and other times we don't, or can't, and yet our bodies remain poised for action.

After a trauma, you may be hyper-aroused (stuck on *on*) or hypo-aroused (stuck on *off*), or vacillate between the two (more about this later). You also may find yourself reacting differently to people or situations. Clients I've worked with who've survived assaults have been scared to tears by a sweet old lady coming around a corner toward them on the sidewalk. Our protective systems can get stuck on overdrive, changing our mental and physical reactions to our environment and sensing danger, even when danger is not there. Thus, we repeatedly brace ourselves for, and react to, an imagined threat.

## Complex Developmental Trauma

What do you call something when it's hard to describe in words? In the case of relationships, Facebook supplies a helpful category: *it's complicated*. Life itself is complicated (as relationships can often be), and so is trauma. It's rare to find a life untouched by trauma, and it's been rare for me, as a clinician, to come across trauma that is unique and specific, without ties to other experiences, memories, or self-perceptions. Complex trauma is a term the clinical community uses to describe what happens when a number of traumatic experiences pile up, interconnect, and complicate each other.

Sandra (I've changed all my client's names here to protect confidentiality) is a client I worked with for a number of years who struggles with a complicated trauma history. She experienced physical abuse at a young age, social challenges during her social development, and sexual abuse in adulthood. Often when we spoke, issues of her family, her feelings about herself, her friendships, and her experience of adult abuse would intermingle, with themes and emotions tying them together even though the original traumas could be considered very different experiences. This is an example of complex trauma. Its roots and symptoms are more complicated than simple, textbook PTSD, which makes treatment more challenging.

Throughout our lives, we continue to develop psychologically, and the developmental stage of the person who experiences a trauma is relevant. Thus evolved the term *developmental trauma*, which highlights this truth and points to the significant impact trauma can have on the many developmental tasks of youth as they develop from infancy to adulthood. The term *developmental trauma* is also unique because it involves multiple or repeated exposure to interpersonal trauma, which describes trauma that occurs in a relationship. Often these types of trauma happens with the meaningful people in our lives – family members, teachers, coaches, etc., although it can at times also involve strangers. Bessel van der Kolk of The Trauma Center in Brookline, MA, proposed Developmental Trauma Disorder (DTD) as a diagnosis in the DSM and continues to advocate for its inclusion (van der Kolk & d'Andrea, 2010). The material we explore in the paragraphs to come outlines his proposed diagnostic criteria.

Developmental trauma can be psychologically overwhelming and difficult to organize, particularly when those who care for you and meet your developmental needs are also causing you harm. Understandably, this creates stress and conflict for those seeking to heal from their traumatic experiences.

Here are some examples of experiences that can contribute to developmental trauma:

- Abandonment
- Betrayal
- Physical assault
- Sexual assault
- Coercive practices
- Emotional abuse
- Witnessing death or violence

These experiences threaten not only our physical but our emotional and social well being. You may notice that each of these challenges, save for perhaps the last one (depending on the circumstance of death), involve the betrayal of trust – trust that people care for us, that they have our best interests in mind, or that they'll be there for us in our time of need. All people, but particularly developing children, need to feel worthy of attention, care, and love. These are the emotional vitamins that help us grow and thrive. Developmental trauma can, therefore, leave deep personal and relational scars that carry forward for years, even generations.

Are you still with me? We're almost through this PTSD overview, so stick with it! When you finish this chapter, you'll be up to speed on the most recent conceptualizations of trauma in the field of psychological trauma and recovery.

Developmental trauma disorder (DTD), as a diagnosis (van der Kolk, 2015), acknowledges that when something happens at an early age it impacts the course of development. When significant layers of trauma occur during child development, it can impact the neurological, emotional, social, educational, and even vocational course of a child's future. Sandra's situation, introduced above, is made even more complex because what happens over the course of her development shapes who she's becoming on many levels.

Here are some aspects of development that this type of trauma can negatively impact:

- Attention
- Attachment
- Mood and emotions
- Trust
- Brain development
- Emotional development
- Social development

If you've worked in the mental health field or with populations at high risk of emotional and social challenges, what diagnoses do you typically see? Can you see how those diagnoses relate to the points above? Perhaps you've served clients labeled with a combination of diagnoses, like Attention Deficit Hyperactive Disorder (ADHD), Reactive Attachment Disorder (RAD), Major Depressive Disorder (MDD), and others. I sure have, so when I read my first article about developmental trauma, it felt incredibly validating. I had finally found the words to describe the complexity of what I'd been working with. This diagnosis gave me the language to describe my felt experience of serving traumatized youth.

I wish that was the limit of the potential effects of developmental trauma, but it's not. Unfortunately, there are other negative impacts of this phenomenon. PTSD is a much more simple, concise and organized diagnosis than complex developmental trauma, which requires more thought and explanation to clarify. This complexity makes treatment and understanding a challenge.

Symptoms of developmental trauma show up across different domains, or layers of being. They can be somatic – occurring in the body – manifesting through posture and sensation. Symptoms can also be behavioral, as is common for those who end up in juvenile halls. They can also be cognitive – impacting ways of thinking, or self-attributional – impacting internal thoughts and feelings about the self. As if all of that isn't enough, developmental trauma can impact relationships, too – their quality, their development, and the way they unfold over the course of a life.

When trauma impacts one's ability to relate, the potential negative implications expand. Experiences of developmental trauma often stem from familial relationships, and they can lead to more conflict and challenges with the family's functioning, even impacting the experience of family upon reaching adulthood. Since trust is directly impacted by interpersonal trauma, peer and even romantic relationships can also suffer. Without foundational social supports in place, social relationships with teachers, supervisors, and law enforcement can also become challenging. Thus, the layers of being potentially impacted by DTD include family, peers, education, vocation, and law (van der Kolk, 2005).

Given all of these aspects of DTD, its complexity can seem overwhelming. How do we provide support and facilitate healing for such complex and deeply interconnected wounds?

Unfortunately, there's yet another layer to address that is common in populations experiencing DTD. Because people who were supposed to help or nurture in the past have not, and trust has been broken one or many times, expectations around support can arise, as can assumptions and expectations around why a supporter is, or is not, present. In the wake of this challenge, the following stances become common:

- Distrust
- Loss of expectation of protection by others
- Loss of trust in social agencies
- Inevitability of future victimization
- Lack of recourse regarding inequalities related to social justice

Often, social, economic, and racial issues also play into the conversation and these topics must be addressed or processed in some way. It is easy to see how someone experiencing developmental trauma can feel overwhelmed by the layers of trauma and systemic challenges surrounding them. As someone seeking to provide support, you will likely feel these same emotions. That's a lot to be up against!

In my opinion, while doing this kind of work as a healer, it's crucial to have support. No one supporter can effectively deal with all the layers of challenge and injustice in the world. We must look to, and form, groups of caretakers that create networks of support – networks that foster resilience so strong that those being served receive the care they've needed and are thus able to experience repair and gain access to sustainable resources. Our foundation *must be* in healing. We need to keep this in mind in order to provide support for those we're serving. It doesn't help if we get sucked into the trauma, poverty, or overwhelm of those we're serving. That would serve no one.

A recent study on adverse childhood experiences (ACEs) surveyed youth exposed to the following experiences and discovered that these adverse experiences can lead not only to emotional and social challenges, but to significant negative health outcomes (Felitti et al, 1998). The more of the following experiences those surveyed reported, the more likely they were to experience disruptions, impairments, risk behaviors, and disease.

- Recurrent physical abuse
- Recurrent emotional abuse
- Contact sexual abuse
- Alcohol or drug abuser living in the home
- Incarcerated household member
- Living with someone chronically depressed, mentally ill, institutionalized or suicidal
- Mother treated violently
- One or no parents
- Emotional neglect
- Physical neglect

ACEs lead to disrupted neurodevelopment, as well as social, emotional, and cognitive impairment. These can lead to health risk behaviors, disease, disability, and social problems, which correlate with risk of early death. It's a really sad story to read about and even more challenging to witness. And yet, this is the truth of early childhood trauma, the truth of how abuse, neglect, untreated mental health challenges, and violence impacts individuals and society.

## Resilience Score

Let's go on to more uplifting thoughts now (hooray!). When choosing my course of study, there was a reason I chose an academic program not focused on sickness, diagnoses, and treatment, but on resilience. I deeply believe in the healing capacity of the human spirit, and I love studying how people grow, transform, and thrive in the face of adversity.

In response to the ACE outcomes mentioned in the section above, psychologists Mark Rains and Kate McClinn developed an inventory to assess for resilience – factors that help prevent those negative outcomes and bolster physical, mental, emotional and social health. The more of the factors in the following list that a child experienced, the more likely they were to be able to access health and diminish the negative outcomes of ACEs.

To get your resilience score (Rains & McClinn, 2013), count a point for every time you answer yes to one of these questions:

When I was little...
- I believed my mother/father loved me
- Other people helped my mother/father take care of me and they seemed to love me
- Someone enjoyed playing with me when I was an infant (and I enjoyed it too!)
- Relatives in my family made me feel better if I was sad or worried
- Neighbors' or friends' parents seemed to like me
- Teachers, coaches, youth leaders or ministers were there to help me
- Someone in my family cared about how I was doing in school
- My family, neighbors, and friends talked often about making our lives better
- We had rules in our house and were expected to keep them

- When I felt really bad, I could almost always find someone I trusted to talk to
- As a youth, people noticed that I was capable and could get things done
- I was independent and a go-getter
- I believed that life is what you make it

Hopefully, the much more uplifting scenarios in this list leave you knowing that there are things that can prevent and mitigate the harmful effects of ACEs. Yes, *you* – as a neighbor, friend, teacher, coach, youth leader, or parent – can have a positive impact on the neurological, social, emotional, cognitive, and physical health outcomes of the children around you. Don't you love this topic? Me, too! We'll talk more about resilience in Chapter 6, so you have that to look forward to.

## Intergenerational Trauma

Someone recently asked me if I believe in the idea that families and ancestors impact our personalities. Absolutely, I do. Science even tells us, it is so. Our genetics, the people who surround us, our environment, and many other factors shape who we are. Recent evidence in the field of epigenetics also teaches us the power of our lived experience. In simple terms, epigenetics is the study of how our experiences impact our DNA. Now that we understand the impact of experience on genes, we know that a child with a high resilience and a low ACE score will pass down a different genetic code to her/his offspring than a child with a high ACE and a low resilience score (Heim & Binder, 2012).

Most parents do the best they can; they take their own experience as a child and seek to improve upon it for the next generation. I've often heard people say things like, "I hated it when my mom hit me, so I swore never to do that to my own child," or, "my parents never had rules and I think it would have done me some good – that's why I make sure to hold the line with my kids." When we carry struggles we're not aware of, or things we avoid, we're passing the impact of these patterns and feelings on to our children. However, when we consciously seek to improve and heal from our own trauma, we're able to improve the cellular information we pass down to future generations.

Children of survivors of the Holocaust, slavery, and other genocides are born with the impact of their parents' experiences in their genetic code. Parents who are more resilient and have access to more healing resources are likely pass the benefits of those factors down to their children, both internally and externally. Along the same lines, a parents hidden scars need not be spoken of to impact or to be felt by their offspring.

What we don't resolve or heal in ourselves, we pass down to our children to sort out. We all carry unique burdens and traumas, as well as unique opportunities for resilience.

## A Heart-Based Definition

Now that we've waded through definitions and explanations of what constitutes trauma, let's summarize and get to the heart of it. Here's a simple description of trauma and its treatment: *Trauma is something that overwhelms one's capacity to cope.* Therefore, we look to build coping skills and resilience to encourage healing. While this simple definition is helpful, the following heart-based description encapsulates, for me, the essence of trauma:

> "Human beings are tender creatures. We are born with our hearts open. And sometimes our open hearts encounter experiences that shatter us. Sometimes we encounter experiences that so violate our sense of safety, order, predictability and right that we feel utterly overwhelmed, unable to integrate and simply unable to go on as before, unable to bear reality. We have come to call these shattering experiences trauma. None of us is immune to them."
>
> -Stephen Cope (Emerson & Hopper, 2011)

I'm confident that, in reading this chapter, you've experienced new insights, discovered new connections, and created new associations – about your own life experience and about the work you do in the world. Whatever pain you have felt, whatever trauma you personally have faced, and whatever those you serve have dealt with, I encourage you to remember that no one is alone. You are not alone, and those you serve need not be. Your journey of healing can light the path for others who face horrific experiences.

Whatever resilience you have accessed, amplify it. Whatever love you feel, share it. And whatever truth you know deep in your heart, speak from it. Don't wait for someone else to give you permission to heal and to shine a guiding light. The world needs the gifts you have, the ones you've filtered from your most challenging experiences. Keep learning, keep growing, and keep sharing. This is what paves the way for a positive future for humanity.

We may not be able to prevent loss, death, or tragedy, but there's much traumatic experience in the world that can be positively impacted by human connection, understanding, and reparative love. While loss is a fact of life, we can shift patterns of abandonment, violence, and betrayal through our choices and behaviors.

As you make your way through the rest of this book, I challenge you to keep in mind questions that orient you toward *solutions* to trauma, rather than the problem. The opposite of violence and betrayal is peace, love, and presence. Ask yourself, "How can I cultivate peace in my life? How can I better love myself and others?" Whatever situation you serve in, ask yourself, "How can I be a force of love in this environment?" The answer is simple, the practicalities complex.

Loving, nurturing and connecting are forces that heal, that bind us to each other, and that help prevent and resolve trauma. So, how do we love in the face of hate, offense, or hurt? How do we love deeply? How do we set boundaries, say no when we need to, and hold people accountable? These questions are worthy of our continued attention. I encourage you to keep them with you as you read this book.

# CHAPTER 3

## Trauma and the Body

In recent years, our understanding of trauma has become more comprehensive – we now know that the body plays a significant role in the healing process. As many cultures and traditions have always known, our bodies and minds are interconnected (duh!).

The field of somatic psychotherapy has contributed much of our understanding of the role of the body and how we can use the body to facilitate deeper, more integrated levels of healing. Although insight, narrative, and other aspects of talk therapy can be helpful, trauma treatment that doesn't address the body in some capacity is incomplete.

Charlie Brown was onto something when he said, "It makes a lot of difference how you stand... the worst thing you can do is straighten up and hold your head high because then you'll start to feel better." Think about how you feel when you stand tall, with your hands on your hips, like the way Wonder Woman stands. It feels pretty powerful, right? What about when you huddle up in a corner and cover your face – how does that make you feel? It makes my mind go straight to a scene of a horror movie!

As someone with a longtime interest in nonverbal communication and in the ways posture reflects our sense of power, it didn't surprise me when I heard about the recent research in "power posing" out of Harvard Business School. What Dr. Amy Cuddy and fellow researchers discovered is that holding powerful postures – any posture that makes you feel physically bigger, like standing with hands on hips, arms outstretched – actually reduces the stress hormone cortisol and increases testosterone, a hormone related with feeling powerful. In the study, it took as little as two minutes of holding a posture for hormone levels to change (Carney & Cuddy, 2010). Charlie Brown's observation, backed by this research, offers an important suggestion to people coping with depression and disempowerment.

Whether or not you have any training in psychotherapy, you may have already been paying attention to the nonverbal communication of the people you serve. Without formal training, many of us notice these things unconsciously. For example, if someone starts to turn away as your conversation stalls, you'll likely to assume they're getting ready to leave. When someone crosses their arms, they may be feeling protective, or they could be physically cold and trying to warm themselves. The way we move in our bodies often tells a story of where we've been, how we feel in the moment, and where we're heading.

Consider, then, how someone with PTSD who's in a yoga class may be challenged to move beyond the physical patterns and structures that express the emotional habits of their being. What they're doing is no small task! As we'll discuss more, changing a physical shape, or experiencing touch, can feel simple to some and can be much more complicated when traumatic experiences are involved.

While working at a therapeutic boarding school in Western Massachusetts, I witnessed students struggle with power posing. As part of graduation, each student gave a speech to the entire group of students and then stood in front of the crowd, arms outstretched, soaking in the applause from peers and staff. This rite of passage was challenging for many of the students. Simply standing up in front of a group to be seen and celebrated was hard enough, but the added physical act of outstretching their arms was no small task. When students were able to do it, they often felt an overwhelming sense of courage and accomplishment. Now we know – they were power-posing! The courage they needed to stand tall not only shifted their perceptions of themselves (I really *can* do this!), it shifted their hormones and stress levels, too.

## The WOT Model

WOT stands for Window of Tolerance, a model of the nervous system developed by Dr. Dan Siegel of UCLA, described first in his book *The Developing Mind* (Siegel, 1999). This model offers insight into how we process trauma, and gives us clues as to how to manage and cope with stress effectively. It depicts the symptoms of a dysregulated nervous system, which hopefully you recognize as one of the challenges of post-traumatic stress. Take a look:

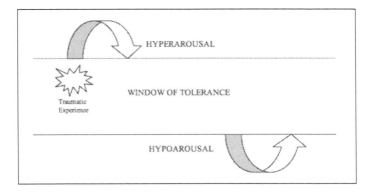

In the center is the Window of Tolerance, which refers to the way it feels when we're engaged with the world, when we can connect and make choices. When we're in this zone, life may feel stressful, but we have access to resources and coping skills that help us manage that stress.

Above the Window of Tolerance is hyperarousal, a state where the nervous system is in in fight-or-flight mode, or sympathetic activation. Here, our system feels stuck on *on*. Another way to say this is that we are activated, meaning that the nervous system has gone into an active mode in order to respond to a real or perceived threat. Yup, even a threat that's not real can send our systems swinging. Have you ever seen a curled-up rope and thought it was a snake? Your body's response in such a case produces a very real surge of adrenaline. Thus, the experience of trauma is much more about the internal than the external experience.

What types of things might one experience in hyperarousal?

The urge to fight or flee, of course, but also the emotions that go along with those options. You might want to punch or scream or run (that's my go-to impulse) or push or shove. It's common in hyperarousal to feel anxious, angry, irritable, or aggressive. Notice what your body wants to do when it's in a state of hyperarousal and can't access resources for coping. Notice the emotions that go with your experiences here.

What pushes us into hyperarousal? Trauma can certainly do so. By definition, when we are out of our window of tolerance, we've lost access to our capacity to cope, or tolerate, and can't access resources that would help us do so. Many experience hyperarousal as the body taking over, and do not feel connected to resources that could soothe the nervous system while in this space.

Most often, when something traumatic occurs we go above the line, to hyperarousal, first. Our systems can stay in this super-charged state for days, week, months, or even years. Alternatively parts of ourselves can hold this energy, and, like an application on your phone taking up energy and draining your phone battery, this energy can tax your energy even when it is not a part of your current conscious experience.

Some people would argue that much of our culture lives in hyperarousal, always reacting, riding stress hormones rather than being reflective and responding. The trouble with hyperarousal is that over time, it's exhausting. We weren't built to constantly fight or flee. When the energy of hyperarousal becomes too intense for too long, our systems often shift below the line and switch to a state of hypoarousal.

Hypoarousal often looks like a body, mind or emotional system that has shut down. It can come with depression, lethargy, isolation, flat affect, and dissociation. Hypoarousal is the home of the freeze response, which is akin to having one foot on the gas (sympathetic activation) and the other foot on the brake (parasympathetic response). The parasympathetic nervous system is in charge during hypoarousal, and it's powerful. We no longer experience a sense of choice, but rather fall into a sense of heaviness or distance from reality that can feel thick and beyond our control to change. We can describe hypoarousal as being stuck on *off*.

The arrows in the diagram indicate the process of healing. While trauma pulls us above or below the line into hyper- or hypoarousal, our goal as therapists, teachers, and in our work with ourselves is to access the tools that will bring us back into the window of tolerance.

## Polyvagal Theory

Dr. Stephen Porges has contributed to recent developments in our understanding of the nervous system, particularly regarding our understanding of the parasympathetic nervous system. His Polyvagal Theory describes two branches of the vagus nerve which correspond with two different parasympathetic nervous system responses. What's most important to know about his theory is that the older physiological response branch (the unmyelinated vagus) dominates with classic symptoms of hypoarousal, like dissociation, depression, and shut down. The more recently evolved branch (the myelinated vagus), relates to social engagement. This is a powerful new insight, and can help us to understand how to access healing.

If the nervous system is dysregulated – in hyperarousal or hypoarousal – social engagement that activates the myelinated vagus can help shift our body's experience from the older system to the newer, more developed version (vagus nerve 2.0, if you will). This explains, in part, why psychotherapy research so often points back to the relationship as a foundational aspect of healing. In this case, social engagement can help us switch from our body's older software to the newer software. This, of course, sounds easier than it often is in practice.

Polyvagal Theory validates an essential, intuitive aspect of healing work. Simply by being you, by being a human being in connection with someone who is struggling to regulate their own system and experience, you provide support and an opportunity for healing, because you are engaging with them socially. Your regulated nervous system offers them a connection, and through neurological mirroring, a shared experience of healing.

My hope is that when you know that posture and body movement have an impact on our emotional and psychological experiences, and that relationships create opportunities for deeply healing nervous system shifts, it will lead you to trust yourself and notice your body more. This knowledge and the awareness you develop can help you to help others. Yes, we still need to learn therapeutic techniques, practice boundaries and be intentional in our work. But, on a deep level, we can also trust our social and intuitive selves to help foster healing.

The beautiful thing about being within the window of tolerance is that's where we connect – internally and externally. It's where we feel that we have options and choices, and that we can access tools to help us cope with challenge. A tool could be as simple as a deep breath, a yoga class, a talk with a friend, or even calling a plumber to fix the problem with the sink. When we're within the window of tolerance, we feel empowered to solve problems, and we're able to relate with other human beings who can help us.

## Top-Down and Bottom-Up Processing

There are many resources for building coping skills to help with recovering from traumatic stress. Breaking these up into two groups, there are two key ways that we can process information that helps us heal. One is called "top-down processing." When we're processing in a top-down way, we're using the mind (in brain terms, the prefrontal cortex and executive function) to teach the body. Most diets are based on a top-down processing model: try to use your mind to decide what your body needs to eat. The problem many people encounter is that this overrides the input of the body. Another approach would be to use a "bottom-up" perspective to tune in and listen to the body to find out what it needs the most. With the diet example, this would mean listening to your body and observing which foods brings it the most energy and how it responds to different foods and activities.

In terms of healing, both of these avenues – top-down and bottom-up – are important. When behavior is out of control, we need to use our brains and get our prefrontal function online enough to make safe choices, like resisting throwing a stapler at your counselor. However, when we go too far and override the wisdom of the body, we can also create imbalances. Many of us who are well-adjusted and socialized to our respective cultures have lost touch with the impulses of our bodies, and this can delay our experience of healing. Being able to allow the body to move and express is an integral part of healing. Even yoga can be more of a top-down practice, with the mind telling the body what to do.

Notice which type of processing you favor, for yourself and also in your work, and invite the question "How can I bring more balance to my approach?" In doing this, you'll strengthen the relationship between the parts of your brain, and between your brain and the rest of your body.

## Body-Based Confidence

Trusting ourselves and integrating information, personal experience, and practice is no small feat. When we feel confident, we communicate it through our posture, voice, and presence. Somatic psychotherapy principles apply to us as yoga instructors, too, of course. When we feel solid about our role as someone holding healing space for others, our clients and students benefit. This doesn't mean we always know the answers or where to go next. Rather, it means we have confidence in the process of the therapeutic relationship and in the capacity of both ourselves and our clients or students.

Laurel Parnell, a leading trainer in the EMDR method of trauma resolution, teaches that if a client senses that you feel on shaky ground, it's unlikely she or he will trust you to hold space for them. But if you feel grounded and trust in the power of your method, clients will jump on board and jump into their process with you. This trust builds a foundation for healing. That trust may even be more important than the healing modality you choose.

Whatever healing method you're offering – be it yoga, EMDR, CBT, or shamanic cleansing – let it be a method you feel confident in. Choose the methods you have the most faith in, based on your studies and experience, and notice how you feel in your body as you propose a specific healing modality to someone. By doing this, you're sharing the faith you feel in your methods with your clients.

We'll talk more about self-care later, but let me bring it up briefly for a moment. Caring for yourself is a way of caring for others. The time, money, and energy you spend on your own personal growth, on your own development, and on integrating the information you've learned into practice, is a gift not only to you but to those around you. Whatever you can do to balance your own nervous system and support your own health is an investment in your role as a space-holder. Do not take this lightly. You deserve all the love you give.

# CHAPTER 4:

## Yoga's Solutions

### Physical Yoga Practice

No question about it, yoga can be a very physical practice. Someone who's not familiar with the layers of depth a yoga practice offers could easily assume that the twisted contortions gracing the covers of yoga magazines define yoga. The most common response I hear when I invite my friends to one of my yoga classes is, "I'm not flexible enough." Can you see their flawed logic? This is like saying, "I'm not fit enough to go to the gym." Yes, yoga has to do with physical strength, flexibility, and agility, but I'd like to offer a broader, more healing perspective about why we practice yoga.

The body is, of course, an important element of a yoga practice. As we've discussed, our physical state can impact stress hormones, feeling states, and have a powerful impact on our minds, emotions, and psyches. The danger of modern yoga is that we become obsessed (as happens so frequently in the modern world) with the external and forget to explore the substance of what's happening under the surface. The goal is to engage with the body in a loving way to build integrated health, rather than sacrificing mental, emotional, or spiritual health in the elusive pursuit of physical perfection.

Sure, a physical yoga practice will make you stronger, more flexible, and better able to balance on one foot (or on your hands, as it may be). You might feel a surge of accomplishment when kicking up into the first handstand of your adult life – as you should (I know, it felt so much easier as a kid). Good for you! It takes courage to challenge the perceived limits of your body. This aspect of the practice can be fun, challenging, sweaty, and rewarding – but the impacts are beyond skin deep.

We've discussed how trauma impacts the nervous system, and this is a key factor when it comes to connecting the physical to the mental, emotional, and even spiritual aspects of our beings. Let's look again at the diagram from Chapter 3 so it's fresh in your mind as we move forward.

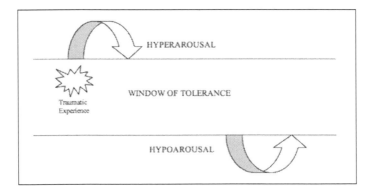

The nervous system is powerful. It relays messages from body to brain and brain to body, swiftly and constantly. When we think of yoga as purely physical, we think of muscles, joints, ligaments, and bones. And yet, as we move those parts of our bodies, we're directing the movements through our nervous system, and using our nervous system to sense our experience. We can use the physical postures and breath to bring the nervous system into balance. How? We'll get to that in a minute. In the meantime, let's set the stage with some yoga philosophy.

## Definition and Philosophy

This is a book about trauma and yoga. We started by defining *trauma*, so let's not go further without defining *yoga*. As you've likely inferred by now (I hope!) I don't think yoga is about contortion, fit bodies, sticky mats, and stretchy pants. Nor do I think yoga is for a particular type of person. Yoga has something to offer everyone. Having studied yoga for almost 20 years now, I have a pretty wide concept of what the practice entails, and I love adapting it to meet the needs of clients I work with.

What does the word *yoga* mean? *Yoga*, in Sanskrit, translates to mean *union, to yoke, or integration*. Essentially, yoga is the bringing together of opposites. Does that make you think of fancy body shapes? Far from it, I hope.

If yoga is a union, a bringing together, of opposites or parts, then what are the parts? This is, of course, open to interpretation. Many would say yoga is about uniting body, mind, and spirit; yin and yang; movement and breath; or attention and time. There are many ways to conceptualize and play with the unifying aspect of yoga's definition. If you're interested, you can explore deeper with your teacher and other yogis how we can embody the profound yet simple practice of union through yoga practice.

If we look to yogic texts, we find more fleshed-out definitions of yoga. The yoga sutras of Patanjali (who was a sage, though scholars aren't sure if Patanjali was a man, a woman, or even a group of people) date back to somewhere between 400 BCE and 200 CE. These sutras, or threads, are short, straightforward messages about yoga that are rich with complexity. Take, for instance, the opening line of the sutras, which translates into English as "Now is yoga" or "Now begins yoga" (Bryant, 2012).

Is this a simple declaration about the book beginning? Or does it more profoundly highlight the reality that *now* is the only moment we ever truly have to act in, so now is the time to yoke opposites together; now is when that union is happening? We're one line into the yoga sutras and it's already obvious how little this yoga stuff has to do with bendy body shapes and nylon pants. Do you already see how much depth there is to yoga? Yes? Good.

Line two of Patanjali's yoga sutras is worth paying close attention to, particularly as it pertains to trauma. The line translates from Sanskrit as "Yoga is the cessation of the fluctuations of the mind." Deep stuff. What would happen if our minds stopped jumping to the past, the future, our grocery list, our life goals, our projections about ourselves and others? A translation of the next line gives us the answer: "Then the seer dwells in her/his own true nature."

Here is what I get out of those three lines: Be present in this moment. Train your mind to be still and you will feel the presence of your deeper spiritual self. We've just taken the fast train from the physical body to a spiritual practice. Awesome! Now let's take a step back and add in the mental and emotional.

Remember how one big problem associated with trauma is experiencing intrusions? Let's explore how yoga can help heal intrusions – thoughts and feelings from another time and space that come into the present – on a mental and emotional level.

## Yoga and the Mind

There are immense benefits to be gained from training the mind to be present. Yogis talk incessantly (I love it!) about where we place attention and about becoming aware of assumptions, habits, and worldviews – particularly the ones that limit us, and their counterparts. Training the mind to become aware of its patterns gives us choices, and choice is a key quality of being in the window of tolerance.

By stilling the mind and focusing on one's breath, a picture, a word, or a feeling of love in the heart (these are not the only options; you'll find more suggestions in Patanjali's yoga sutras), we become aware of how much our minds are constantly working overtime, and we're able to repeatedly make the choice to bring ourselves back to present time and space. This allows negative patterns to lose their charge. We're also able to be aware of what our minds are being pulled toward – the stories and quirks that live below the surface of our daily to-dos.

Years ago, while sitting at a ten-day Vipassana meditation retreat, I began to recall food commercials from the early 1980s and crave foods I hadn't eaten since I was a child. I was a vegetarian at that time in my life, but I experienced cravings for non-veggie foods that were so intense I was certain I'd go home and eat a ham and cheese sandwich and inhale some peanut M&M's – all childhood comfort foods. But by the end of the retreat, those cravings (which had been quite an unexpected intrusion) had moved and gone away. The feelings passed, but the experience stuck with me.

A client recently said to me, "It's incredible what the brain can hold," and I couldn't agree more. You have your own early childhood songs, commercials, cravings, and more – all stored up there in your brain – along with memories, self-concepts, and imprints left from various experiences. Indeed, the brain holds more than we're aware of when our attention is constantly busy with the responsibilities of daily life. Mindfulness practices, be they yoga or seated meditation, help us to uncover these habitual grooves in our minds and make choices about our thoughts and behavior. Yogis call these grooves *samskaras*, and we find them in the mind and in the body. A yoga practice helps us become aware of our physical and mental habits and, over time, change them.

## Yoga and Emotion

It *is* incredible what the mind can hold, and the same is true of the heart. Our hearts can hold much more than we're aware of. Emotions play a part in yoga and in healing from trauma. Most people who have symptoms of intrusions will not resolve those symptoms by simply practicing mental presence (though it can help, particularly practicing thought-stopping or orienting when in crisis or in a hyper-vigilant state). Experience has taught me that intrusions come as a result of unprocessed emotion. The solution, naturally, is to find ways to process that emotion. Luckily, as I like to say about all kinds of things, #yogaisgoodforthat.

There are many ways to process emotion – talk to a friend, notice the story that the emotion creates, make sense of an experience, complete unfinished responses, move the body, emote, or even pray through the discomfort. For many of us living busy Western adult lifestyles, it can feel that we don't have the time or energy to tend to our emotions. It's common for us to ignore, sweep away, and repress our feelings, avoiding them (notice the similarity to PTSD) or hiding them under a pint of Ben & Jerry's ice cream. I'm all for self-soothing, but when emotions stick around too long without actually being tended to, they can take on a life of their own and, if left unchecked, draw us into repetitive behavior patterns that suck the joy from our lives and prevent us from healing.

## Big Feelings

When an emotion is not conscious we act out how we're feeling – like kids often do. That feeling then becomes part of our experience in the physical world. Rather than staying internal, the feeling morphs into a dynamic in a relationship, a problem at work, or a physical manifestation of stress. What yoga offers is a space to let emotions surface, ideally before they create behaviors and situations in life that lead to suffering.

My favorite yoga sutra is in Chapter 2, line 16: "Future suffering can, and should be, prevented." A physical yoga practice aligns the body to prevent injury, builds awareness of mental habits, and provides space for emotions to move so they aren't unconsciously acted out. This is like regularly straightening the living room or taking out the trash. I often offer clients an emotion/dishes analogy, asking them, "Would you leave egg yolk on a plate for a week? No? Then why let anger or sadness sit without attending to them?" The analogy holds over time, because the longer we avoid the cleaning up that needs to happen, the more solid it becomes and the harder it is to clean up and start fresh. It's sill possible, it just takes a little more energy.

This may be a new way for you to look at yoga, that the pose is more about the emotional process than the physical result. Focusing only on the physical postures, we can lose sight of the fact that early yoga texts talk mostly about seated poses, not about cranking your leg behind your head. There's nothing wrong with developing flexibility in your hamstrings and hips (please don't forget the quads, the neglected stepchild of modern yoga), as long as it's done in a way that doesn't bring harm to the body. But – news flash – not everyone's body can do every pose, even when they're in great physical shape, and many people do themselves a disservice trying to force a yoga pose that goes against their anatomical structure. If you or your students have been pushing the physical aspects of yoga without practicing ahimsa (nonviolence), bring it back to the asana, which translates as seat, and sit your lovely self down. It's often in the stillness that we become aware of more subtle emotions, sensations, and intuitions and provide space for our emotions to process and clear.

Now that you are seated on the cushion, notice how you feel. Meditation can be powerful and especially challenging for those dealing with PTSD, so be gentle with yourself and practice what is tolerable each day. Sitting to meditate as part of a yoga practice gives us the opportunity to feel and make our way to the other side of deeper emotional experiences, so try on short sessions at first to see how it goes for you. Remember, *the slower you go, the faster you get there.*

Many different qualities have shown up for me in day-to-day meditation. Sometimes my mind is busy and full. On other days, I feel dull, uninspired, sad, or long for someone or something. Other times, I have to keep a notepad nearby to capture the creativity that starts to flow when I sit. On days where I feel overwhelmed, I often pick a simple word to repeat in my mind, or open my eyes and focus on a still point (based on the layout of my home, I often end up gazing at my steel water bottle on the kitchen counter).

The point here is that moving, breathing, gently challenging your body, and cultivating mindful awareness can help us feel our Bigger Feelings. I capitalize Bigger Feelings because it's important – there are layers of feelings and it can take time and effort to excavate and understand them. "Why did I feel lonely then?" "Why did I act out of anger toward that person?" These are all questions worthy of exploration. Perhaps more importantly, worthy of space in our lives. Yoga carves out this space, in both its dynamic and its still aspects.

If you have yet to read Candice Pert's book *Molecules of Emotions*, I highly recommend that you get on it. In it, Pert explains the biology of emotion. Her research helps to clarify the relationship between neurological processes, emotion, and the more esoteric healing processes. Understanding these relationships helps us soften any mind-brain-body barriers we've created by putting ourselves, our thoughts, and our feelings into boxes to better categorize our experiences.

## Koshas

Yoga sees the body differently than Western medicine, mapping it in sheathes or energetic layers called *koshas*. The concept of a layered presence of being might feel more natural to you than mental-emotional-physical self divided into boxes. Explore this way of relating to yoga, your body, and your emotions. I find that each client I work with has a layer they're more in tune with. Notice what you feel most connected to. One of my yoga teachers, Patricia Walden, often says that we use the body to teach because we all see it and can mostly agree on it. We all have bodies, but we all have different experiences of life. With physical asana, it is easy to direct someone to put an elbow in a certain place. You have an elbow, I have an elbow, and we can both see the spot on the floor I'm pointing to. However, as things get more mental, emotional, and subtle, our ability to communicate shared ground becomes more elusive. This is perhaps why the physical body has become a primary focus of the yoga practice in Western society. And that's okay – it gives us a window onto the whole, a way to begin seeing that these layers of our being relate to one another.

## Spiritual

I often find myself asking, "What does the word *spiritual* mean?" I see spirituality translated into yoga practice in a multitude of ways, some of which deeply inspire me, and others that feel false, limiting, or simply not right for me.

In this physical realm, we search for words, but all too often they fall short. Different spiritual communities have different and specific ways of viewing life experiences. In contrast, the beauty of a yoga practice is that you can decide for yourself what the spiritual aspect of yoga means for you, based on your experiences.

For me, the phrase from the yoga sutras, "the seer dwells in her own true nature" resonates, maybe because I've heard and read it so many times. It speaks to the essence of the life inside, the part of us that's not our job, culture, ethnicity, economic status, looks, gender, sexual orientation, status, etc. It defines *spirit* as our essence, what's there after all else has been stripped away. A local yoga teacher here in San Francisco often closes the class by saying, "When I am in that place in me and you are in that place in you, we are one." It's a beautiful sentiment, one that speaks of this union that yogis often report experiencing after a deep yoga practice.

Many spiritual belief systems focus on oneness, on the interconnection and interrelations of all beings, everywhere. This can be a lot to chew, and recognizing our relationship to each other, to the Earth, to the past and the future, can be hugely humbling. An awareness of these relationships can help us make choices in the present moment that bring the most benefit to ourselves and others.

A simple, accessible way I define spirituality is "being in tune with yourself and your interconnection with life." It's important for each of us to ask ourselves what makes us feel alive, expressed, and connected. Whatever brings you a sense of deep passion and purpose can also bring you closer to a sense of flow or connection with something divine.

So, what connects you to your own spirituality? Do you feel connected to a religious or secular belief? For some people, quantum physics is spiritual. For others, God, Jesus, Kuan Yin, the Virgin Mary, Mohammed, Mother Earth or the Universe symbolizes spirit. Define spirituality for yourself, and if none of the external symbols apply, look to your experience in yoga. Do you experience an energy or a self beyond conditions when you practice? How would you describe your deepest meditation or savasana? That description can give you a strong clue about your experience of divinity and can help you explore the unexplainable realm.

## Layers of Practice

What I love most about a yoga practice it that it addresses all of these layers and leaves room for you to choose (window of tolerance!) what works best for you and to explore what you feel drawn to at a deep level. There's no wrong answer in this realm of exploring, and you only answer to yourself.

Yoga philosophy does make some assertions, but they're not there to be forced on you. They're there for you to ponder, to reflect on, and to chew on. Curiosity allows you to question the assumptions you have and to make choices that align with your deepest sense of self. That, to me, is the essence of spirituality – to self-express and connect, to see our own unique beauty and share our light with the world.

As Marianne Williamson says in her book *A Return to Love*: "It is our light, not our darkness that most frightens us... And as we let our own light shine, we unconsciously give other people permission to do the same. As we are liberated from our own fear, our presence automatically liberates others" (Williamson, 1992).

Shine on, friend.

## Yoga Philosophy and the WOT

One of the wonderful things about yoga is that because of its long lineage, we have the benefit of ancient wisdom passed down to us. Although the Window of Tolerance model is relatively new, there are qualities of nature described in the Bhagavad Gita that mirror this model and can help us conceptualize how to use yoga poses in an intelligent, balancing way.

The Bhagavad Gita introduces the gunas as qualities of nature. Gunas are not good or bad, they're simply words that describe qualities that exist in the body and in the world. There are three gunas: *rajas*, *tamas*, and *sattva*. Rajas has the quality of movement, athleticism, energy; rajas has a fiery nature. Tamas is heavy, dull, lethargic, still. Sattva is a balanced state where there's a steady steam of energy and attention just enough to meet the moment and be present to it. Sattva is a state of calm, clear, connected presence.

Whether or not you decide to share the concepts of the window of tolerance or the gunas with your students or clients, it can help you to keep both the developing science and the ancient wisdom in mind. They can inform our perspectives about human physiology and encourage us to find balance instead of residing in extremes that tax our bodies and minds. Consider how you can weave these ways of understanding into your offering of healing. Consider also how this can help you stay healthy, grounded, and sustained in a way that allows you to remain energized and connected to your work.

# CHAPTER 5

## Resilience

When we talk about healing, it's important to orient ourselves toward what we're fostering, rather than toward the pain or challenges we've been exposed to. It's essential to ask, "What are we creating?" as we work toward a deeper understanding and integration of traumatic experiences. Although it can be an important piece of healing to tell our stories and process the negative emotions and beliefs that arose from them, it's crucial to be rooted in health while doing so.

## Resilience

I've seen clients who've exhausted their healing efforts. They've been to therapists, shamans, acupuncturists, and biofeedback practitioners, and completed endless courses and exercises in efforts to heal. I applaud their drive, but find it interesting that when I ask them about what they're cultivating with their healing work, they often they fall silent and don't have an answer. It's so obvious, once you see it, but many of us miss this crucial step. It's important to process negative emotions and experiences *and* build a platform of resilience. If we get stuck or lost in either, our experience is incomplete.

Clinicians often describe trauma as a vortex of energy. Indeed, trauma can have a strong pull and it can feel incredibly challenging to become free of its hold. The experience of trauma's energetic pull can be quite strong, so let's take a moment to connect instead to an image or a feeling of healing.

Focus for a moment. Stand or sit tall, align your head and your heart, and notice your breath. With your eyes softly gazing at these words, call to mind an image or a feeling of healing that resonates with you. This could be a peaceful scene, an animal that represents healing, or a place in your body that feels safe, comfortable, or inspired.

I have many of these images and feelings, one is Kalalau Beach in Hawaii, on the island of Kauai, where I was lucky to spend spring break during my freshman year of college. Together with a group from UCLA, I hiked twelve miles to this remote beach. When I go here in my mind, I can smell the guava trees and the blue-green ocean water, see the whales breaching the waves, hear the sound of the ocean. I feel peaceful. Another resource I go to is a feeling I can only describe as a waterfall in my heart. Sometimes, at the end of a rigorous yoga practice, I emerge thirsty, with a deep feeling of love and energy pulsing through my heart center. The sensation I call having a waterfall in my heart is like a thirst and a quenching at the same time.

Each of those thoughts, when I think them, take me to an imprint of the positive experiences I've had. They not only remind me that my life has not been all bad, they also offer a window into healing and connect me to positive emotional experiences I hold in my body. Doing this – tuning in to positive memories and experiences – can shift our biochemistry. I call these positive memories and experiences I've identified *resources*. Developing your own and calling on them can help you build mental, emotional, and physiological resilience. They build a platform of resilience that can help with healing from trauma. If you'd like to learn more ways to practice resourcing, check out my book *How You Can Heal: A Strength-Based Guide to Trauma Recovery*.

Resilience can show up in many ways. It can be a deep impulse to bounce back, a slow effort to make meaning, a commitment to building coping skills, or simply a desire to feel better. While some people conceptualize resilience as something we either have or don't have, we can all access resilience and build it through practice. Rather than wonder whether or not you're resilient, ask yourself how you can develop resilience and how you can help your yoga students find resilience – not only physically, but in other layers of their being. Explore to find approaches that help you build up your resilience reserves.

## Resilience and WOT

Let's look back again to the Window of Tolerance figure we discussed in Chapter 3, Trauma and the Body.

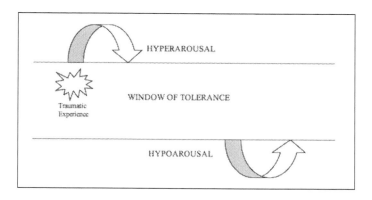

What images, feelings, memories, or imaginary experiences (movie scenes, fantasies, etc.) connect you to your window of tolerance? What takes you into the range where you can connect with others and feel calm, empowered, and soothed? Asking yourself these questions will help you build your resilience and widen your window of tolerance.

Trauma and extreme stress causes the window of tolerance to narrow. We've all had experiences of snapping at someone who didn't deserve it, or of not being able to tolerate simple stresses when sh*t is really hitting the fan. Building up our resilience, coping skills, and capacity to be present in the moment helps us widen our window of tolerance, stay self-regulated, and maintain access to choice.

## Wise People

When I was growing up, I met many of my mom's colleagues. My wise and wonderful mom, Noonaheeyot (I have no idea how she got this name) is an excellent trauma therapist, and her colleagues are similarly so. As a teenager, my bullshit detector was good (as I'm sure yours was), and I recall telling my mom, "I like your colleagues. They keep it real." The reason I felt so comfortable with those trauma therapists was that they, by trade, had had countless opportunities to widen their window of tolerance. They were wise enough to know what to react to and what not to react to, and it was hard to shake them. Show up with a tattoo, a piercing, and a mouth full of f-bombs? No problem, they were comfortable with that (not that I tried all those things myself). I had the felt sense with these people that I could not shake them with my behavior, which reduced any tendency I may have had to be a mischievous teenager. They had earned a widened window of tolerance and because of that, I felt comfortable being myself around them. Their wisdom was likely part innate, part learned through the challenging practice of treating complex trauma.

I bet you've known a person so experienced in this life that no matter what news you bring them, they're not surprised. This is one indicator of a wide window of tolerance. Wise people often have a way of knowing the parameters of life – its scope of joys and horrors – in such a way that whether you tell them you won a million dollars or your dog just died, they can respond with love. This is self-regulation. This is having a wide window of tolerance. It doesn't mean they don't feel excitement or sadness, it just means that they don't become swept away by their emotions and that they've identified supports to ride the waves of their physiological responses.

Wise people are settled within themselves and can stay grounded, present, and self-regulated – even when you are not. They can hold space. Wise people know that your issues are yours, and they increasingly build their awareness so they don't act out and dramatize big feelings. By not reacting, by pausing and making conscious choices in thought, word and behavior, they allow the people they come into contact with more of a chance to recognize what they're doing, even subconsciously.

Notice what it's like the next time you're in the presence of someone who can hold space. What do they do when you share that you're sad or angry? What do they do if you try to take out your frustration on them? Compare their reactions to someone whose window of tolerance is narrower, who overreacts or shuts down. Notice the difference in your experience and notice how your relationships with wise people develop.

I want to clarify that I am, in no way, saying it is bad or wrong to not have a wide window of tolerance. It's is, however, much more comfortable to be in the window – and it's much more challenging, painful, and disruptive to relationships to be outside of the window. We all have moments where we get dysregulated, but the more we each work to regulate ourselves, the more we can support one another in coming back into the window, a space where we can connect and choose, a space where we feel integrated and connected to ourselves.

When something life-changing happens, as can be the case with trauma, our window can widen, either immediately or slowly with the healing process. Take, for example, losing a loved one. My experience was immediate in that things that would have stressed me out and sent me swinging before the loss no longer held any weight for me. It was a reorganization of my values and priorities. In such a reorganization after a trauma, simple daily stressors can become meaningless. Ten minutes late to a meeting? In the big picture, that's not life-changing. For some people, it can be easier to cope with the minutiae of life when there's big emotional digestion taking place that shifts our perspective.

Think of your own experience and the experiences of the people you serve. When does the window of tolerance get narrow? Is it when stress is stacking up, when blood sugar is low, when a specific relationship is stressed? When does the window of tolerance widen? Is it after yoga class, in the wake of loss, when your best friend is around? Begin to think of not only what gets you into the window of tolerance, but what widens your window and allows you to hold more space for yourself and for those you serve. Knowing what regulates you helps you access your own resilience.

## What do safety and recovery look and feel like?

One of my clients recently made me aware of a question I often ask: "What would that look like?" Until she pointed it out, I hadn't realized how often I'd asked her to use her imagination to pave the way forward into the look and feel of the life she wanted for herself, internally and externally. When she shared that after hearing that question so much from me she'd begun to ask it to herself, I realized that I often ask my clients to explore what safety, recovery, healing, and resilience look and feel like to them.

While I could go the metaphysical route to explore techniques of manifestation, I'll stick to my area of training and expertise – mental health and psychological resilience. If you know what you're looking for, you're much more likely to find it. Have you ever dropped a contact lens? Anyone who has can attest to the level of faith and certainty it takes to locate the lost lens, because of how challenging it can be to find, even when it could only physically have fallen within a few square feet of floor space.

What I'm interested in, as a psychotherapist, is not precisely what life will look like in a material way, but what it will feel like to be living a life of resilience. Often when we allow our minds to drift in this manner of imagining what we want, we connect with the parts of ourselves that crave happiness, health, and fulfillment. Creating those feeling states is more important than getting specific about the material aspects of what we want.

External specifics can, however, help us identify the feeling states we want. To use a tangible example, think of your ideal new car. Marketers are already working hard to sell you feeling states, so get in touch with the feeling the new car brings you. Do you feel successful, attractive, organized? Explore the external thing and the feelings it brings, then let the specifics of the external circumstance fade. Now do this with your future, healed self. What does healing feel like? You may not know, but it is worth exploring and imagining. This orients your subconscious mind and helps you to notice the choices that will take you closer to the feeling state you're aiming for.

## Neuroplasticity

Doctors and scientists used to believe that the brain was fixed. It was created, it grew to a certain fixed state, it deteriorated, and died. Now, thankfully, we know that the brain is much more active and responsive to behavior and to the environment. Thanks, also, to functional magnetic resonance imaging (fMRI) machines, we can see the brain's activity as it responds to stimuli and adapts over time. We call this responsiveness *neuroplasticity*, meaning that the brain has a plastic, or shapeable, capacity. Studies show that mindfulness practices, like yoga, can prevent the decline we used to take for granted as part of the brain's life cycle (Khalsa, 1998).

You've likely heard that memory games and exercises can help "keep the brain young." My 100-year-young grandmother would agree that you've got to "move it or lose it." Something else you might have heard is "neurons that fire together wire together," meaning that when we think about or initiate new behavior, new neurological impulses are created, and the more we repeat them the more we build that new neural network in the brain. Established neural pathways make behaviors easier. Let this principle work to your advantage – choose thoughts and behaviors that create networks of healing in your brain. This helps to offset negative symptoms and speed recovery from trauma.

## Principle in Practice

Some of you who are reading may be circus freaks (like my mom) who can do just about any contorted thing with you body one can imagine. The exercise I'm about to offer may be an old hat trick for you. However, for most of us, doing such things with our body is profoundly difficult.

Lets try something. If you're comfortable with it, take off one of your shoes and your socks. Go ahead, I'll wait (unless it's un unresolved trauma trigger, in which case, please keep your shoes on, get the supports you need to ground yourself, and continue reading when you're ready). Now that at least one foot is bare, take a look at your big toe. Wiggle your toes a little. Feels nice, right? Most shoes are too tight anyhow. Now, look at your big toe and give it a wiggle, but don't let any of your other toes move. If you're like me (and it still happens for me, even though I've had some practice with this), the other toes are simply too eager to come along for the ride. If the big toe moves, so do the other toes. If you feel so inclined, try both feet. An Iyengar yoga teacher in one of my recent workshops could do this (it's possible!), but she said it took her *ten years* of regular practice. *Ten. Years.*

I give this example for a variety of reasons. Primarily, I want to show you that, while neurological re-patterning is possible, it's not necessarily easy. When we tell someone in an anger management class to take ten breaths before making a choice about whether or not to punch someone, we might as well be telling them to wiggle just one toe. Taking ten breaths and making a responsible decision may be easy for us, but we've had years of practice at it, and our brains are wired to even unconsciously practice thoughts and behaviors that bring calmness in the face of anger. However, for someone who hasn't had such neurological training from teachers, parents, and caregivers, or who's experienced a trauma that's rewired their brain, we're working with neuroplasticity to create new neural pathways. Possible? Yes. But it takes a lot of repetition, reinforcement, and practice.

## Post-traumatic Growth

An aspect of resilience that's specific to trauma is the growing understanding of post-traumatic growth. Post-traumatic growth (PTG) as a field emerged from studying people who felt not exclusively negative in the wake of traumatic experiences, but who also had positive developments in their lives. This does not negate the fact that having an experience of trauma is shitty. It does, however, highlight that good can come of even the crappiest of experiences, and many people find, create, or experience silver linings around even the darkest clouds in their lives. There are many ways this will occur. In the following five sections, I highlight five common themes of PTG.

## Personal Strength

One of the outcomes of post-traumatic growth is personal strength. When we go through something that, at one point in time, felt impossible to survive, and we find a way through, this gives us proof of our own fortitude. Personal strength is often hard earned, through the development of the skills, attitudes, and practices of resilience, and through following the thread to find what brings us healing. Whatever we've digested, healed, and integrated emotionally gives us evidence of our strength. That strength can help us in the face of other adversities. The fact that we lived and coped with the trauma is testament of our strength, even when there's still emotional work to do.

## New Possibilities

When trauma arrives, it can shake up our lives, our expectations, even our sense of self. This can, naturally, be upsetting and off-putting, but it can also create new opportunities. It's unlikely that I would have such an intimate knowledge of trauma if I hadn't lost my brother when I was in my early twenties. Sure, my mother is a trauma therapist and, sure, I've studied the crap out of psychology, resilience, and trauma. My traumatic experience led me to not only do deeper relational work, but to seek and forge the path of my own healing. As a result, I can draw on studies, the experiences of my clients, and my own brushes with trauma. Although I wouldn't wish any of my own traumatic experiences on anyone, they did create new possibilities – new ways for me to connect with people who are experiencing various forms of trauma, and to help them.

## Relating to Others

My experience of traumatic loss created an opening for me to relate to those who were experiencing a range of types of suffering. While someone else's suffering may not be from the same circumstances as mine was, our felt sense was similar enough, and, through that common ground, we could connect.

Two of my primary yoga teachers had histories that paralleled my own, but I didn't find that out until years after my intensive times of studying with them. I didn't find them by reading about their histories and then showing up knocking at their doors because I thought that they would "get" me. Yet, in their presence I felt their understanding. I felt seen and safe. I felt that they had navigated through deep challenges and emerged resilient, integrating their stories rather than suppressing or managing them, and that sense of recognition – even though I didn't know any details – connected us.

## Appreciation of Life

Trauma often exposes us to the fragility of life, and thus it can lead us to a deeper appreciation of being alive. The number of times I stop to smell a flower these days is ridiculous, given how busy I am, but I make time to appreciate small moments in my day. I also have a deep appreciation for the value of people. Given my exposure to traumatic loss – personally and in my work – I know from experience how precious life is, how quickly it can go, and that our unique selves can never be replaced. Recognition of deep truths such as these can change our relationship to the gifts we have in each present moment, and connect us to a sense of gratitude for what we still do have.

## Spiritual Change

Many experiences of trauma involve loss or a brush with death, and this can give us a new perspective of life. After experiencing a trauma, many people shift their perceptions to include energy, symbolism, mysticism, or spirituality. For some people, deep spiritual experiences are intertwined with their trauma (as in near-death experiences). It's common for people to report a deep and lasting change after a trauma, and to seek out a new or renewed path of spiritual development as a result of their experience.

*⁓•⁓*

We often think of resilience as bouncing back, and often conflate the term with not being impacted by pain or trauma. The type of resilience I see most often, however, is a slow, steady commitment to rebuilding life and exploring oneself in the wake of traumatic experiences. While there are some uncontrollable factors that influence resilience, there are also many choices we can make that help us to heal, to reformulate our lives and ourselves in a way that enhances life more than it depletes it. Through resilience, we can take the puzzle that was soaked in water and put through the blender, and create a Monet.

# CHAPTER 6

## Trauma and Relationships

### Attachment

Human beings depend on each other; we are interdependent physically and emotionally. *Attachment* refers to a deep and enduring emotional bond that connects one person to another across time and space (Stayton & Ainsworth, 1973; Bowlby, 1969). Young children are dependent on caregivers to meet their needs. For this reason, attachment between parent and child has become a significant area of focus and research within the field of psychology. However, attachment is also a factor in friendships and romantic relationships and can even emerge between colleagues who work closely together and interdepend on each other.

There are many ways to study attachment and observe the impacts and challenges of attachment. For the purposes of this book, I'll focus on healthy attachment. Remember that we want to build our foundation in health, not disease or disorder. Healthy attachment between caregiver and child, and in other types of relationships, necessitates a level of connection and reciprocity. The capacity for each party to attune to the other is essential. When we feel a sense of shared experience, we feel more connected.

Dr. Dan Siegel of UCLA outlines four components of relationships that can encourage healthy attachment. He calls these the four S's: When individuals feel seen, safe, soothed, and secure, they're more likely to develop healthy attachment (Siegel & Bryson, 2011). Feeling that another person gets us, respects our bodies and emotions, can talk us off a ledge, and will be there when we need them are crucial components in relationship.

In addition to those four qualities, I like to add another s: *stable*, meaning that there's a predictability in the other person's responsiveness, a rhythm within our interactions, or a felt sense we have that tells us that person will be there for us when we need them. Even if you go long periods of time without connecting with someone you have a healthy attachment to, there's a depth and durability in the connection that lets you know you can always reach out to them.

Think about the people you feel most connected to or attached to in your life. Which of those people make you feel seen, safe, soothed, secure, and stable? How would you rate the quality of those relationships? Can you see the difference between those relationships and your relationships with people you're connected to but who don't foster those feelings in you? It's a different feeling altogether, isn't it? Consider, as well, how you hold space for the people you serve, because you're in a position to build a healthy relationship dynamic with them.

We'll talk later about shame and how fostering connections within which someone can feel seen, safe, soothed, secure, and stable can help prevent shame spirals, which are a significant emotional risk related to trauma. This is important information for all of us to be aware of, for ourselves and for those we serve.

## Attunement

What does it mean to feel seen? Often it's a sense that the person across from you really gets you. Some of this feeling comes from their ability to attune to you and take in your perspective. We know how painful it can feel to be misread or misunderstood, and yet we may not consciously recognize the degree to which we feel seen by others, although we often choose relationships based on this feeling.

Let me give you a concrete example. Before a show, musicians often play simple games, like catch. Why would doing that be more important than spending that time tuning their instruments or going over their plan for the show? Musicians are in a relationship with each other as they play, so their ability to attune to the other band members is essential. They need to be open and connected to each other so that if someone improvises or makes a mistake, the others can respond to it. If you're a musician who plays music with others, think about how you attune to your bandmates, the conductor, the audience. You feel into another person's space and respond to it, often subconsciously. This is attunement.

Another example of attunement is when a mother learns just what a baby needs. That knowing may be based on the tone of the baby's cry, the mother's integrated knowledge of baby's schedule around their physical needs, or the mother's close attention to subtle shifts in baby's mood, behavior, and expression. When a mother has this skill, it's very helpful for the child, as it means the child's needs are more likely to be met. Most mothers also have the strong bond of having carried their child inside the womb, sharing space so closely that their biologies are intimately connected. The more connected we are with another, the more we can pick up on their patterns and cues and the better we can respond to them.

Entrainment is a concept in physics that explains what happens when two interacting systems assume the same rhythm or period. Essentially, they impact each other until they're in sync. The word period lends us to the example of women in close quarters ending up on the same menstrual cycle. While more research needs to be done in this area, this could be when bodies, or perhaps hormonal systems, become entrained. Another common example occurs when two people in conversation take on mirroring postures or positions, in essence, joining one another to become part of a synchronized system.

Do you recognize entrainment of some kind in any of the relationships you've had? My study and experience of working with and in relationships for the past fifteen years tells me that *entrainment* is a good descriptor of our experience of relationships. Tightly knit couples become very well entrained. We hand the keys to our partners just as they begin to look for them. We finish each other's sentences. We share ideas, sometimes without even speaking. One person calls the other right when the other person picked up the phone to call them. We feel connected through entrainment. Entrainment is another way to conceptualize how we connect and impact each another when we become attached.

Recall our discussion of developmental trauma and how that's related to interpersonal relationships and betrayal. There is all kinds of research coming out these days on the impact of a broken heart on our physiology and stress levels. As anyone who's been through heartbreak knows, the experience is intense and painful. When relational bonds have been broken, it can become difficult to trust others, which can lead to isolation or a feeling of not getting our relational needs met. We are social animals. We survive in relationship and some of our most basic needs depend on the actions of others. Though many Western cultures promote individuality, the truth of life is that we thrive in balanced, healthy relationships.

## Shame Resilience

Trauma can bring about a significant experience of shame. Recovering from shame happens best in a relationship, by telling others about the things that make us feel bad about ourselves and having those things be met with love. Brené Brown asserts that shame cannot survive being spoken and met with empathy. She describes four steps in shame resilience: Know your shame triggers, reality-check them, reach out to someone you trust, and tell your story (Brown, 2013). It's important that we choose wisely who to tell our stories to, so that we're met with empathy. A rupture in trust can decrease our ability to recover from shame.

There's great value in having even one emotionally safe relationship where you can expose shame and have it be met with love. Who are those people in your life? Also be aware of the value of your presence when someone trusts you enough to share their shame with you.

## Safe Relationships

I told a boss I had once that I "didn't feel safe" when talking to a coworker, and then realized that I needed to define the term *safe*. I didn't mean that I thought my coworker was going to hit me, stalk me, or assault me in any physical way; however, I did feel that she would attack me verbally and become defensive if I brought my concerns about her to light. I didn't feel safe to express myself or confident that my needs would be considered or responded to responsibly if I did express myself.

Emotional safety is crucial in healing work. It builds trust and the capacity for interdependence. Learning to identify who in their life feels safe can be a challenging process to go through for many trauma survivors, yet it's an essential part of recovery, as it precedes building trust in a conscious and healthy way. Encourage those you serve to determine how they know they feel safe with someone and what they need in order to feel safe, if they aren't feeling it yet. Know that this process can be long and can require exposure to new and unfamiliar dynamics in a relationship as the survivor learns how to identify a safe relationship.

## Relationship Repair

John Gottman, an expert in couples counseling who is famous for his ability to predict a couple's likelihood of divorce within minutes of watching them interact, said, "Mostly, all you can do in love is repair how you screw up" (Gottman & Silver, 2015). No relationship is perfect. It's silly to expect that you'll never piss off your partner, other members of your family, or your best friend. The effort required of you, then, when something goes awry, is to apologize, communicate, reach out, and repair that relationship. Hashing out disagreements and challenges to the point where you can say, "Are we good?" and the answer is, "Yes, we're good" is crucial to maintaining love and connection. Letting things fester is not productive. Remember the egg yolk on the dishes analogy. That's a recipe for relational residue, which leads to a felt sense of disconnection.

As attuned, present, and loving as you are, you can never fully step inside another person's experience. We will make mistakes. The sooner we can own up to them and reach out to repair them, the better for all involved. This rebuilds the relational platform and allows us to move forward. It also requires humility, openness, and acceptance of our mistakes. Consider how you can weave the freeing energy of relationship repair into the way you hold space for yourself and others.

## Competing Interests

I've heard competing psychological interests defined as *a concurrent drive toward protection and resolution.* As much as we seek to grow, there is a pull to stay the same. Donald Winnicott, an influential psychoanalyst in the field of object relations theory, described this push-pull feeling throughout his work as a deep part of ourselves that is both hiding and desperate to be seen. He famously said, "It is a joy to be hidden, and disaster not to be found" (source unknown).

What's at risk when we grow, stretch, or put our true selves out in front of others? What's at stake when we step into the next phase of our development? These questions can help us identify our internal barriers to growth. Simply showing up and talking to someone, saying something out loud, can be a step toward growth, toward being seen and heard.

Notice within yourself where conflict exists between the urge to protect yourself and the desire to grow, and also be open to how this issue may be influencing the souls you serve. Don't underestimate the power of your open heart and ears, of your presence and your capacity to witness others as they stretch into the unknown. For yourself, find those gems of people who you can speak your tentative hopes to in safety. They are your tribe, and there need not be many of them to have a profound impact on your life.

# CHAPTER 7

## Teaching to Traumatized Populations

When teaching to traumatized populations, there are important factors for you to keep in mind, many of which will be unique to the people you serve. All of the chapters above build a foundation of understanding that helps you relate to the people you serve and the beneficial processes you're teaching. Keep in mind that modeling these practices is as essential as instructing them, and that your relationship with your students can help guide you to discover their specific needs and respond to them.

## Coping with Red Tape

If you want to teach yoga in a school, correctional facility, nonprofit, or recovery program, you need to be ready to deal with red tape (if you don't run into any, celebrate(!!) and skip this section). As yoga becomes more accepted as a therapeutic tool, you'll hopefully have a smoother time offering your gifts to those who can benefit. However, if you're in one of the many places in the world where yoga isn't understood or celebrated, read on, my friend, and we'll prepare you to cope with institutional red tape.

The first thing to rely on to feed your capacity to face the slow pace of bureaucracy is your own yoga practice. Call on the very same mental strength and patience that gets you through a long hold of pigeon pose and that keeps you patiently practicing your balance poses away from the wall. Whatever your physical practice, call on the patience, dedication, and commitment you bring to it, and take that strength and experience with you into any challenging conversations you have with staff, program directors, and funders. Be kind to yourself, gentle in the process, and consistent with your goal.

Things that are new can feel unfamiliar, unknown, and bring up fear. It's natural for people to be hesitant if they don't understand what you're offering or how it can help. Although you are well-versed in the benefits of yoga, those you work with or want to work with may not be. Learning requires repetition, so you may need to say the same things multiple times to help people understand. Patient, non-reactive repetition can be helpful in skirting judgments and negative attitudes. This gives you an opportunity to put your yoga skills into practice yet again. You can practice responding rather than reacting, and by creating enough space for yourself, you can to avoid the temptation to take the negative beliefs or projections of others personally. Of course, this is easier said than done. Like a yoga practice, it takes consistent effort and commitment to your outcome. Keeping in mind your goal of offering yoga to those who need it will help.

In addition to finding ways to cope as you navigate through red tape, you can be strategic with your language. Notice what will serve the program best and, rather than describing yoga from your own perspective, describe it using words that the program will understand. Terms like "stress management," "self-regulation skills," and "symptom reduction" tend to do a better job of convincing program decision-makers than "asana" and "pranayama." Consider how you can meet the needs of the staff, and include them in your goal-setting for the program. In addition to using the theory and practical suggestions in this book in your proposals, search for and include research that's specific to your population.

## Becoming Aware of Enactments

The power of pain is strong, and it can affect all who are in its presence. Unresolved, misunderstood feelings often play out in behavior. When we're dealing with trauma, there are, by definition, overwhelming feelings in the mix. This is why resilience and orienting to healing are so crucial. Build a platform of healing resources for yourself, and have supports in place that you can rely on. If you're not well-resourced, you may begin to feel the way your clients or students do: overwhelmed and without the skills to cope.

We've discussed the trauma vortex, enactments, and how situations that don't stay contained within one person come out in behaviors in relationship. If you're doing trauma-healing work, these things will happen to the people you're helping. The key is to look for them and to become aware as soon as possible that they're happening. A great way to do this is to use your own emotions as a guide. Notice how you feel before you step into your role at work, in a session, or in a class. Notice how you feel during and after the interaction. The impact on you of the client, student, or group will show up during and after you spend time with them, and you may find that you have all kinds of reactions to your experience. Some of those reactions will have to do with your own issues, like how you treat yourself and think about yourself while you're teaching or therapizing. Also, if you do something that feels out of character, or if you feel an emotion that's rare for you and feels hard to trace, this may be part of an enactment. You can use that information.

Often, our clients (particularly teens and children) pull out our parenting instincts, and we may find ourselves wanting to take them home to take care of them. Alternatively, we can get sucked into behaving with them the way other adults have with us. Make sure you have support that helps you notice how you're different with different people, and what that means for you. Use the yogic concept of *svadhyaya*, or self-study, to reflect on your behaviors. Ask yourself, for example, "Why did I make this choice with this particular person?" Gathering this type of information can help us get clearer on what the client is experiencing, and helps us stay connected to our own true experiences rather than acting out someone else's habits or challenges.

## Minimizing Vicarious Trauma

To minimize your own vicarious trauma, seek to become aware of enactments and the power of the trauma vortex. Learn about not only what happens to you when you know you're burning out, but what happens when you don't know you're burning out, and have a support team that can help you recognize and communicate the signs.

Find your rituals, the activities or behaviors that help you process what you're going through as you do this healing work – like a run, a yoga class just for yourself, or a shower after work. At a clinic where I worked I used to joke that we needed a big green showerhead in the hallway –- the kind used in science labs for emergencies after chemical exposure, because whenever I returned to the clinic after doing my work outside the clinic, I felt the desire to cleanse myself of the energy of struggle, disappointment, grief, and trauma that I'd been not only exposed to, but steeped in. Sometimes, a ritual as simple as washing your hands or changing clothes can help make the transition from work to home, to feeling that you have a healthy boundary between your personal and professional experiences. Search for a way to help you clear and cleanse at the end of a long day of service.

## Cultivating Safety

There's a practice in yoga called *pratipaksha bhavana* – which means *exploring the opposite*. We can use this practice to develop flexibility of mind. It comes in particularly handy when we're stuck in a negative thought loop, as happens in most cases of post-traumatic stress.

Applying this practice to trauma leads us to ask: What is the opposite of trauma? Since trauma often involves loss of control and lack of safety, we can cultivate their opposites by holding safe space for those recovering from trauma to explore having choice in their bodies.

How can you cultivate safety in your classes? How can you give students and clients a feeling of control over their own experience? Creating group rules generated by the students can help create a space where people have what they need. Offering those you serve choices is a key piece of allowing them to have control. No yoga cults, please! Offer your students and clients the opportunity to choose for themselves. By doing this, you demonstrate that you respect their individual needs and experience.

One way to cultivate safety is to help students in a yoga class feel physically safe. This promotes a calmer nervous system and reduces the risk of people with PTSD becoming triggered. It's important to consider the layout of the class and how you have people arranged. When people can see their surroundings and each other easily, and there's a clear line of sight between teacher and student, that will help. Allow students and clients to have a view of the room's doorways, and leave an open path to these doors, so they see that they can leave if it becomes necessary. Having an open door policy that allows students and clients to leave the room if they need to is best, though it may not be feasible in inpatient or incarceration settings.

Teaching yoga in a space that's contained is helpful, meaning that there's a defined scope to the space, rather than a big, undefined openness. A feeling of containment can also come from minimizing interactions with other groups during class; for example, not having the class overlap with other activities that could be distracting. I've taught yoga in places where there is a basketball game happening on the other side of the room; while it's better than not having yoga, it can interrupt the sense of containment for the group. Having a predictable structure for the classes and a holding classes in the same space also contribute to a sense of familiarity, which will allow the nervous systems of the participants to feel more at ease.

Once you've set up the class environment, protect and enhance your space. Consider ways you could minimize distractions and interruptions. You may choose to cover mirrors or have a silent cell phone policy. Extreme temperatures can be stressful for the body, so keeping the room at a moderate temperature can help the body's systems feel regulated.

It's key to set up your space in a way that creates a felt sense of safety, so come back to this issue repeatedly. Ask those you're working with for their input on what class structures would make them feel at ease. Consider, as well, what you can do to build a felt sense of community. How can you cultivate healthy connections between your students? How can you celebrate their gifts and resilience? This doesn't mean that everyone needs to be in each others' business, but that you foster a culture in which everyone is equal and belongs in the space.

As we've explored, many people who have survived interpersonal violence find it hard to build safety in relationships. It may be challenging to create trust or to feel seen. Although we'll never be perfect, our efforts are important. Being honest, authentic, and responsible helps to create safety and trust in our relationships with survivors. Being willing to apologize and admit to making mistakes also goes a long way in building trust and an equal sense of worth with participants.

It's essential to practice presence with difficult emotions, rather than reenacting a trauma response of avoidance. In this type of work, difficult emotions arise. Know how you handle your own emotions and rely on your own resources, so that you can be a role model for others and remain non-reactive, yet responsive, when big emotions fly.

## Play, Joy, Celebration, and Rest

The opposite of being unsafe is to be safe, but there are other opposites of trauma we can consciously cultivate. The opposite of being frozen in terror is to be fluid, playful, dynamic, and joyful, exploring freely and without fear. In the initial stages of trauma treatment, those aspects of life can feel worlds away. In those times, focus on safety and containment. Once you've established a safe foundation, keep going. Encourage your students to move with less rigidity, to be fluid and playful, and to explore what, in yoga and in life, brings them a sense of joy.

Balancing rest and activity is a central concept of many religions and health approaches around the world. Notice the way you teach regarding activity and rest and how they balance. Explore your teaching style. Do you tend to favor activity or rest? Many yoga practices in the West are skewed toward overworking. If you find that this is true of your teaching style, ask how you can encourage rest and rebuilding. Both energies are important aspects of healing.

# CHAPTER 8

## All About *You*

### Passion for Work

For those of us who do this work, it can be easier to refer
to the collective opinion and overlook your own role and
experience. But if you're wading through the trenches of
trauma and working with trauma survivors, it's important
to be clear and connected to yourself. What is your *why*?
Know this. Motivation is as key in this field as in any other,
and even more so, given the difficulties we can be up against.

Live your purpose as a meditation. We talk about challenging poses, about sitting and bringing your attention back to
the present and to the breath, about feeling the full range
of human experience – joy, grief, anger, silliness, frustration, rage, excitement. These are all practices that help us
better cope with, respond to, and engage – not only with
our work and with PTSD survivors, but with *life*.

When you've become still enough and clear enough to
know what's important to you, what you want to create
and experience in your lifetime, what will leave you on your
deathbed not without regrets but feeling satiated and sat-

isfied – *do it*. We want to think that when we've found our soul's calling the roads will clear and everything will align in divine order to support us. Sometimes that happens. Other times, we struggle. This is part of the human experience.

Like birthing a child, following your soul's calling will involve contractions and pushing, moments where sensations are overwhelming, and moments of rest and even ease. No birth, no life, is identical. Do your best to allow the temptation to compare fall into the background as you engage with your life.

The closer you get to those big feelings of success and satisfaction as you follow the path of living your purpose, the more you may experience the challenges of distraction, confusion, and fear. Keep unpacking the feelings and refocusing on what has the most meaning and energy for you. Yes, this often means letting less important things fall away.

The biggest gifts have the most wrapping paper. Remember that. If you have a lot of love to give, there's a chance that there's also some fear there, some self-doubt or hesitance surrounding your sweet, gooey, wonderful heart. Removing the wrapping can take a long time (or, if you're Burt from Sesame Street, a big pair of scissors). Have the courage to unwrap your gifts.

## Boundaries

I'm still learning boundaries. I'm such a yes person. Yes, we'll make it happen, Yes, I'd love to speak at that conference. Yes, I'm going to write a book about trauma and yoga (oops, how'd that happen?).

Right now, as I pour myself into this book and this effort to integrate yoga and trauma recovery, I'm not the best example of setting limits. Seriously, I'm writing this at 11:29 p.m. while at a conference in upstate New York that I paid my own travel expenses to attend, volunteering a week of my time to help write best practices for teaching yoga to veterans. Did I mention that I'm sitting in the bathroom here at the hotel because my roommate is sleeping? I'm so passionate about this work that everything else fits into the cracks around it. It's comical for me to stand up on a soapbox about boundaries right now, and yet, it remains a practice for most all of us in this line of work.

I'm working on the issue of boundaries with you, teaching what I need to practice – as many of us do. While I wouldn't change my decision to be here, in this bathroom, writing to you, it does make me recognize the ways I need to set limits in order to preserve my energy for the long haul. Marathon training is great practice for this; rather than sprint a mile, I'll continue to make choices in my life that create a balanced pace, overall.

Please, for the love of all things holy, do whatever you need to do to identify and communicate your boundaries. I am right there with you in this effort.

## Personal Life

While boundaries are challenging for me, I'm actually pretty good at having a personal life. Losing my brother, who I was so close to, when I was in my twenties, taught me how precious our time here together is, and that people are what's most important. So I prioritize spending time with friends, even when it means traveling to them or clearing space from work to be with them during important moments of their lives.

I encourage you to do the same, to take a hard look at your values and how you spend your time. The tricky part of this is that most of us who work with yoga and trauma do it because our desire to help in this way comes from deep within our hearts, and so the boundary between work, play, and personal pursuits can be blurry. Where are those boundaries for you? Do you have ways of turning your professional life off? Who helps you realign your perspective if you get pulled into working too much?

## Nature's Gifts

A growing body of research shows how healing it can be to be outside, close to nature, immersed in the elements. The good news is that you don't need to live near a beach or hike up the tallest mountain to find relief in nature. Doing something as simple as walking under the trees at a local park, lying on the grass in your backyard, or even tending an indoor garden can connect us to nature (and provide us with more oxygen). Particularly if you're a city-dweller, make sure you get regular doses of nature. Consider how you can expose your clients and students to natural experiences and themes.

## Play for *You*

In treating trauma, we seek to create a safe physical, mental, and emotional space to foster healing, but what happens once we've accomplished that goal? Do we just sit in safety and comfort ourselves? Safety is the foundation, not the end point. Since trauma disrupts this foundation, we must seek to repair the foundation first. When the base has been built, or repaired, we can continue to create.

It can be difficult to explore play and celebrate when we're responding to and recovering from trauma, but doing so can be healing and can build a bridge into a way of being that's fluid and resilient. All too often when dealing with mental health treatment, we lose sight of the medicinal qualities of awe, play, fun, and celebration. We forget that reducing negative symptoms is only half of the process. The other half is connecting with joy.

Think about where you are in your career now. Whenever I've come to the end of a stage of my own career, what I've been doing that used to bring me intense joy starts to feel heavy. I've tested my interest, tried to problem-solve and push through, but the sensations in my body and spirit tell me it's time to move on. And the longer I resist, the more painful it gets.

What stage are you in with your work around trauma healing? Where does your work feel inspired? *Follow that.* Let inspiration lead the way, whether that inspiration is to serve in the same way or a different way, whether it's to take a break and deeply care for yourself. Follow the inspiration rather than, for example, a fear of not having enough money or not being good enough at whatever it is you want to do next. Cultivate a vision of your work and its evolution while also being open to things unfolding differently, as they sometimes (and, in hindsight, quite magically) do.

# CHAPTER 9

## Sustainability

Teaching yoga to traumatized populations can be hard work, and yet you wouldn't have gotten this far in this book if you didn't feel called to do it. Your purpose and passion will fuel you, but please know that you can't do this work alone. Create a structure of accountability, support, and community for yourself that allows you to reflect on what you're doing and improve your skills over time. This evolution is part of what keeps you in the game – able to thrive as you continue to serve.

When you're surrounded by people who care about you, love you, and want you to feel happy, you have not only their support but their eyes on you and their willingness to comment on your behavior. "Do you need to do this?" "Why are you working on Saturday?" "It sounds like it's time to set a boundary." A supportive community (which doesn't have to be a large number of people) feeds your self-care practice in that it helps you become aware of when you're in danger of burning out.

## Avoiding Burnout

One of the best interview questions I was ever asked was asked by the woman who became my supervisor: "What happens when you don't know you're burning out?" Rather than giving her examples like noticing I'm not going to yoga classes as often, or I feel cranky all the time, her question called me to reflect on the times I'd been side-swiped by vicarious trauma and became tired before I had the awareness to respond to my own needs. Her question stayed with me and keeps me returning to this issue to make sure I have resources set up around it.

Supervisors, I encourage you to ask this question to individual and groups that you lead. Everyone else, don't wait for someone else to start this conversation. The more you talk about this to yourself and with your community, people at home and at work, the more equipped you'll be to keep yourself in the game and care for your own needs as they arise.

## Who Am I?

Another reoccurring theme I've witnessed in this work has to do with the question, "Who am I to do this work?" It can be easy to feel like you need another degree, or you need someone to validate the fact that you're a healer, or that you'll wait to start until you have better, faster, sharper internal or external tools. Yes, of course, it's important to continue to learn. But be careful about selling yourself short.

Many of the skills we use as healers, such as empathy, attunement, and connecting with others, are god-given. This doesn't mean you should work without a license or certification, but it does mean that at a certain point, enough self-doubt is enough. You have what you have today to give. You'll gain skills and experience by engaging with the work in front of you, by seeking support for challenging issues and problems that arise, and by showing up after a setback to continue to serve – perhaps accompanied by tears of loss, an apology for a mistake, and a celebration of success. Keep showing up and doing your best. That's something you can do and it's big. It's enough.

If I wasn't modeling this leap of faith, you wouldn't be reading these words right now. If my editor hadn't been on my ass for me to finish this book, I would have pulled an Axl Rose and taken eleven years to create this "album" so that it could be released into your hands. Don't be that guy or gal who gets in your own way. Don't wait for that elusive, non-existent perfection. Give what you can today, offer the wisdom you've already collected, give the gift of your presence, and allow yourself to grow into a better service provider.

## Money

In addition to burnout, self-care, and self-doubt, money is another hot topic in service work. Here's my recommendation to you: Participate in the economy. You deserve to make money doing healing work. Think of how much time, energy, and effort you've invested in your own growth, learning, and healing. It counts for something! Decide how you want to give back in the form of volunteering or reduced-rate work and then make sure the rest of your working life is sustainable financially.

Charge what your sessions are worth based on how much value – how much love, energy, and compassion – you bring to your clients and students. I know you bring oodles of attention and care to your people, and I know it's hard to put a price tag on intangible things. I bet you wish money was not an issue and you could offer your services for free. But money is an issue. The people we serve often get more out of our services if they've invested in them. We can't ever know the full benefit of how we help people, of the people we've helped going on to live their lives from a healthier place. Do yours clients and students a favor and challenge them to invest in themselves. They are worth it, and the more healers we have with abundant bank accounts, the more power healers will have in the marketplace. Claim that power, and decide how you can best give back in a sustainable way. Remember, no one can get on your life raft if it's sinking!

⌇

Gina (her chosen pseudonym) is a yoga teacher I've worked with for many years. She's been through all of these struggles, at one time or another. She tells me that having support has made all the difference. Before we worked together, Gina felt that she couldn't assert her boundaries, since many of the people she was working with had trouble doing the same. In order to care for herself, she had to break through the expectations and group norms in her environment that set people up for burnout, resentment, and, eventually, disengagement.

It was only when Gina pointed out the cycle of burnout that others spoke up to share their needs for more sustainable income and energy. It often takes at least one person breaking an unspoken code of silence to begin to shift a culture in a positive direction. It can help to get perspective from someone who's outside of your system.

You having support can make all the difference, in your life *and* in the lives of those you serve.

# CHAPTER 10

## Moving Forward

Here we are, at the end of our journey. We've waded through definitions of trauma, discussed the functions of the nervous system and how trauma impacts it, explained how standing like Super Woman changes our hormones, and explored the healing capacities of yoga. We've discussed the importance of building a foundation of healing, of creating healthy, helpful relationships, and of continuing to do our own work as providers of healing spaces, so that we can support ourselves and continue to thrive.

My hope for you, dear reader, is that this book has offered you inspiration to be a force for healing in the world, and that you continue to do the important work you're called to do.

There are more people looking to recover from trauma than there are people offering solutions. The knowledge you now hold can support many others in their healing process. Don't be shy! Don't wait until you know everything. There will be mistakes and learning along the way, to be sure, but I urge you not to wait.

There is, there will always be, so much more to learn. You can learn even as you help from who you are now and what you know now. Teach everything you know now. Offer the love and insight you feel now. Look for and find the ways that serving in the world lifts you up and go there, do those things with and for the people you feel called to serve.

## What to Do Next

Find the places where your love and service will be received and go there. Find the places where people celebrate the gifts you bring, the places where you feel you can have an impact. Find the people who are doing similar work. Create community together and support each other.

Claim your own power. Uplift others. Those you serve will go on to hold space for others. This is how we create positive change in the world. This is how we foster peace. This is how we create much-needed healing momentum in the world.

We can never have enough healers in our midst.

## Stay in Touch

People like you who are called to serve and to offer opportunities for others to heal continually inspire me. I would love to hear from you as you work to integrate this information into your own practice of yoga, therapy, and healing work. I invite you to stay connected by joining me on Facebook or Twitter, and by going to my website to watch my free training videos I offer and get the latest news: **howwecanheal.com/y4t.**

For those of you wanting more support, information about my in-depth Yoga for Trauma (Y4T) online training can also be found on my website. If this speaks to you, reach out to me to and we'll explore how you can get involved.

I look forward to hearing from you and send you all my love and support.

# REFERENCES

American Psychiatric Association. (2013). *Diagnostic and statistical manual of mental disorders (DSM-5°)*. American Psychiatric Pub.

Bowlby, J. (1969). Attachment and loss: *Attachment* (Vol. 1).

Briggs, B. (June 20, 2014). DOD and VA Can't Prove Their PTSD Care is Working, Study Claims. NBC News.

Brown, B. (2013). 3 Steps To Break The Cycle of Shame. Retrieved from: http://www.huffingtonpost.com/2013/10/08/brene-brown-shame-oprah_n_4059675.html.

Bryant, E. (2012). Yoga Sūtras of Patañjali.

Carney, D. R., Cuddy, A. J., & Yap, A. J. (2010). Power posing brief nonverbal displays affect neuroendocrine levels and risk tolerance. *Psychological Science*, 21(10), 1363-1368.

Caruso, K. (2015). PTSD and Suicide. Retrieved from: www.suicide.org/ptsd-and-suicide.html.

Casey A.E., & O'Hare, W. P. (1994). *Kids Count Data Book: State Profiles of Child Well-being*. Annie E. Casey Foundation. Retrieved from: childhelp.org/child-abuse-statistics.

Emerson, D., Hopper, E., & Levine, P. A. (2011). *Overcoming trauma through yoga: Reclaiming your body*. North Atlantic Books.

Felitti, V. J., Anda, R. F., Nordenberg, D., Williamson, D. F., Spitz, A. M., Edwards, V.,... & Marks, J. S. (1998). Relationship of childhood abuse and household dysfunction to many of the leading causes of death in adults: The Adverse Childhood Experiences (ACE) Study. *American Journal of Preventive Medicine*, 14(4), 245-258.

Gottman, J., & Silver, N. (2015). *The seven principles for making marriage work: A practical guide from the country's foremost relationship expert*. Harmony.

Harris, N. B. (2014) The Chronic Stress of Poverty, Toxic to Children. Shriver et al, *The Shriver Report*, 204.

Heim, C., & Binder, E. B. (2012). Current research trends in early life stress and depression: Review of human studies on sensitive periods, gene–environment interactions, and epigenetics. *Experimental neurology*, *233*(1), 102-111.

Khalsa, D. S. (1998). Integrated medicine and the prevention and reversal of memory loss. *Alternative Therapies in Health and Medicine*, 4(6), 38.

Rains M. & McClinn, K (2013). What's Your Resilience Score? Retrieved from: https://acestoohigh.com/got-your-ace-score/.

Siegel, D. J. (1999). *The Developing Mind* (Vol. 296). New York: Guilford Press.

Siegel, D. J., & Bryson, T. P. (2011). *The whole-brain child: 12 revolutionary strategies to nurture your child's developing mind.* Delacorte Press.

Stayton, D. J., Ainsworth, M. D., and Main, M. B. (1973). Development of separation behavior in the first year of life: Protest, following, and greeting. *Developmental Psychology*, 9(2), 213.

Tanielian, T., & Jaycox, L. (2008) Invisible Wounds of War Psychological and Cognitive Injuries, Their Consequences, and Services to Assist Recovery. Retrieved from: www.rand.org/content/dam/rand/pubs/monographs/2008/RAND_MG720.pdf

Van der Kolk, B. A. (2015). *The body keeps the score: Brain, mind, and body in the healing of trauma.* Penguin Books.

Van der Kolk, B. A., & d'Andrea, W. (2010). Towards a developmental trauma disorder diagnosis for childhood interpersonal trauma. *The impact of early life trauma on health and disease: The hidden epidemic*, 57-68.

Williamson, M. (1992). *A return to love* (p. 165). New York: HarperCollins.

# THANK YOU

Thank you for reading this book.

This book is a launching point. You now know more than most people do about trauma and yoga, but there is more to learn, integrate and apply. There is more theory, research, and practice to consider, but I also plan to continue to write and offer you more opportunities to embody these principles.

As my gift to you for making it through the book, I'd like to offer you a free four-part video series on yoga and trauma. This series offers more specifics about poses – both how to do them and their impact on the physical and emotional body. You can access the free Yoga for Trauma (Y4T) video series at **howwecanheal.com/y4tfree**.

You can find a more in-depth online training opportunity at **http://howwecanheal.com/y4t/**.

I'd love to know how this work develops for you! Please feel free to contact me with questions, ideas, or stories you'd like to share. You can reach me at **howwecanheal.com**.

**Stay Connected**
Website: www.howwecanheal.com
Facebook: facebook.com/lisadanylchukmft
Twitter: @lisadanylchuk
Instagram: http://www.instagram.com/howwecanheal
Google Plus: Google.com/+LisaDanylchuk
YouTube: youtube.com/c/LisaDanylchuk

# ACKNOWLEDGMENTS

I cannot say thank you enough. Thank you, thank you, thank YOU.

Thanks to my UCLA roommate Kristy, for connecting me with Kathleen Harper who led me to Angela Lauria and Grace Kerina – the midwives of this book. Thank you, Grace, for holding me to deadlines, and to Angela, for encouraging me to get something out there and publish it rather than waiting until I had all the information ever possible included in this book (first pancakes are quite tasty).

Deep gratitude to my yoga teachers, Gianfranco Amaduzzi, Patricia Walden, Seane Corn, Laura Miles, Lisa Walford, and all the other teachers and students I've learned from, practiced with, and played with (Carrie Owerko!). Thanks to Hala Khouri for letting me assist your workshop umpteen times, and to all the healers I've worked with, crossed paths with, and taught. I'm grateful for your love, your presence in my life, and your presence in the world.

I'm grateful to have such loving, supportive parents. My mom and dad are incredible human beings and magnificent parents. Mom, Dad, I thank you for always supporting me in following my heart (to Tibet, Mongolia, Haiti, Peru, etc, etc). Your commitment to growth and love are palpable. Thanks to my brother Mike, for making me laugh on the regular and for reminding me daily that brilliance comes in many forms (mostly yours). Thanks to my

Grandparents who have passed, Homer and Barbara, Peter, and to Grandma Peggy, 100 years old as I write this, for your positive, independent spirit. From you I've learned to make the best of each day.

Thanks to all my homies in the Mateo – you know who you are (#Weenies4Life). Thanks to my college roommates and dear friends; to my HGSE advisor, Dr. Mike Nakkula; and to Dr. Josephine Kim and Dr. Holly Lem. I'm forever grateful for your wisdom, caring, and tireless support. Thanks to my fellow R & P alums, who are all so, so badass. Cheers to all the amazing work you continue to do in the world. Thank you to my running family for keeping me (in)sane. I hope you all know how much joy you bring to my life!

Thank you to every client I have ever worked with. Your courage and tenacity has inspired me more than you know. Thanks to the youth at Nickerson Gardens Housing Development in Watts for inspiring me to march forward in the face of challenge, for allowing me into your homes, and for sharing your Janet Jackson dance moves with me. You are brilliant and amazing and worthy of every bit of good the world has to offer. Should we cross paths anytime soon - yes, I still have gum in my car, and yes, you can have some.

This list of thanks would not be complete without acknowledging and celebrating the life of my brother Matt, whose beginning, middle, and end taught me to recognize the depth and capacity for love that existed within my own heart. I love you eternally, brother.

Thanks to any and all spirits, ancestors, guides, angels, muses, and anonymous flutters of inspiration, for helping with this book and much more, for sticking around, and for being good company. A deep bow to you and to all gods and goddesses of healing and light.

To each of you who are reading this, thank you, too. Now go spread some love!

# ABOUT THE AUTHOR

Lisa Danylchuk is a psychotherapist and yoga instructor who is passionate about integrating yoga into trauma treatment. For over fifteen years Lisa has served as a therapist and yoga teacher in juvenile halls, prisons, schools, non-profits, and community programs across the US. Lisa earned her undergraduate degree at UCLA and completed her master's work and advanced studies at Harvard University. For the past ten years she has been researching, writing, and presenting her work to mental health providers and yogis around the world.

Motivated by her passion to increase awareness and provide education about trauma and recovery, Lisa serves on the UN Task Force for the International Society for the Study of Trauma and Dissociation (ISSTD) and on the board of Your Strength to Heal (YSTH), an organization serving survivors of trauma and sexual exploitation.

Lisa is a licensed psychotherapist and a Yogaworks Certified Yoga Instructor, and loves encouraging healing through yoga and mindfulness. Beyond healing, she seeks to support people in creating joyful, meaningful lives, and to uplift themselves while uplifting others.

For more information, go to **www.howwecanheal.com**.

Difference Press offers entrepreneurs, including life coaches, healers, consultants, and community leaders, a comprehensive solution to get their books written, published, and promoted. A boutique-style alternative to self-publishing, Difference Press boasts a fair and easy-to-understand profit structure, low-priced author copies, and author-friendly contract terms. Its founder, Dr. Angela Lauria, has been bringing to life the literary ventures of hundreds of authors-in-transformation since 1994.

---

### LET'S MAKE A DIFFERENCE WITH YOUR BOOK

You've seen other people make a difference with a book. Now it's your turn. If you are ready to stop watching and start taking massive action, reach out.

"Yes, I'm ready!"

In a market where hundreds of thousands books are published every year and are never heard from again, all participants of The Author Incubator have bestsellers that are actively changing lives and making a difference.

"In two years we've created over 250 bestselling books in a row, 90% from first-time authors." We do this by selecting the highest quality and highest potential applicants for our future programs.

Our program doesn't just teach you how to write a book—our team of coaches, developmental editors, copy editors, art directors, and marketing experts incubate you from book idea to published bestseller, ensuring that the book you create can actually make a difference in the world. Then we give you the training you need to use your book to make the difference you want to make in the world, or to create a business out of serving your readers. If you have life-or world-changing ideas or services, a servant's heart, and the willingness to do what it REALLY takes to make a difference in the world with your book, go to http://theauthorincubator.com/apply/ to complete an application for the program today.

# OTHER BOOKS BY LISA DANYLCHUK

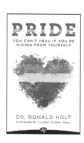

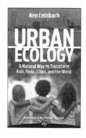

*Flex Mom: The Secrets of Happy Stay-At-Home Moms*

by Sara Blanchard

*Your First CFO: The Accounting Cure for Small Business Owners*

by Pam Prior

*Just Tell Me What I Want: How to Find Your Purpose When You Have No Idea What It Is*

by Sara Kravitz

*From Sidelines to Start Lines: The Frustrated Runner's Guide to Lacing Up for a Lifetime*

by Sarah Richardson

*Everyday Medium: 7 Steps to Discover, Develop and Direct Your Sixth Sense*

by Marsha Farias

*Think Again!: Clearing Away the Brain Fog of Menopause*

by Jeanne Andrus

*Relationship Detox: 7 Steps to Prepare for Your Ideal Relationship*

by Jodi Schuelke

*Unclutter Your Spirit: How Your Stuff is a Treasure Map to Your Inner Wisdom*

by Sue Rasmussed